Brian Godfrey was born and br
leaving school spent five years on
and attended engineering colleges at Welwyn and Hatfield.

He played a good standard of football and represented Essex at Boxing, but at the age of twenty-one he joined the Merchant Navy in an engineering capacity.

He later transgressed into the world of nuclear submarines and then into the Oil and Gas industry where he travelled extensively in a management role, representing both contractor and then the client.

Now retired, he lives in Hertfordshire.

ALSO BY THE AUTHOR

The Compassionate Terrorist

UMTATA

BY

BRIAN GODFREY

A sequel to *The Compassionate Terrorist*

Matador
9 Priory Business Park,
Wistow Road, Kibworth Beauchamp,
Leicestershire. LE8 0RX
Tel: 0116 279 2299
Email: books@troubador.co.uk
Web: www.troubador.co.uk/matador
Twitter: @matadorbooks

ISBN 978 1838591 403

British Library Cataloguing in Publication Data.
A catalogue record for this book is available from the British Library.

Printed and bound by CPI Group (UK) Ltd, Croydon, CR0 4YY
Typeset in 11pt Baskerville by Troubador Publishing Ltd, Leicester, UK

Matador is an imprint of Troubador Publishing Ltd

PROLOGUE

WINTER 1980

It is sad to know of homeless people, those who have no place to go, no family to care, and little chance of a meaningful future. They 'make out' somehow, scrape by and exist with little hope.

Spare a thought for those who wake up, a cold wind at their backs and nothing more than an old blanket or duvet for warmth. They are the lucky ones; others, less fortunate, have nothing.

There are no career opportunities, no end-of-year bonus; their only possessions are the clothes on their backs and a pile of dirty bedding; their home is the local park, or a bus shelter, or at best warming themselves over a kitchen grill at the side of a hotel.

These are real people; they want a change for a better life. Excluded from civilised society, old, young, sane or unstable, educated or not, there is no conformity; life carries them into the future without a goal.

But there is a light at the end of the tunnel, and that is to survive!

1

THE START OF A NEW LIFE, NOVEMBER 1980

The night sky was clear, the stars twinkled; it was perfect, and the only distraction was the noise of the endless London traffic forever moving through the busy streets. The wail of a police siren momentarily broke the monotony; none of the passers-by looked up or took any notice, it was normal. The pavements were crammed with people, some hurrying about their business whilst others played with their mobile phones. Some, unfortunately, had nothing – no phone, nowhere to go. These were the destitute.

Few alternatives were available to them – perhaps a visit to the local supermarket, only to gaze at food; or to feel the hot air from the extractor fan from a local restaurant, its warmth and subtle smell radiated into the night. With nothing else to do but throw a duvet into some street corner, cover their heads to conceal themselves from the world outside and sleep, lights, however bright and twinkling, were not welcome. The darkness was better, where the CCTV cameras could no longer watch their every move.

The evening was slipping away, but under those neon lights walked a lonely man. He walked under cover of the doorways, aspiring to be anonymous but looking conspicuous; warm coat, a woollen hat pulled over his head, blond hair protruding over his collar – only a ray of light showed his light blue eyes behind his thick-rimmed glasses. Lean and athletic, he walked on his toes – like a gazelle, not the gait of a vagrant. The collar of his dark blue jacket was pulled up around his neck, and it would not be difficult to guess that this man had something to hide.

Shivering in the cool evening breeze, the cold was getting through to his body; he felt weak but needed to be positive. He started to walk more briskly, then slowed his pace; there was no reason to go fast, nothing to speed up for, nowhere to go, at least not tonight. Though he was exhausted, it did not deter him from appreciating the city's buildings – the old with the new, the past with the future. This architecture could tell a million tales; but to investigate these tales was low on his agenda.

He had survived over four months since absconding from his job in the Shetlands, a fugitive no nearer to where he wanted to go, no closer to another identity, no closer to peace. He had enjoyed his life in the north, and none of those people he had worked or socialised with had suspected that either his friend Declan McBride or himself were associated with terrorism. Mixing amongst everyday folks, they kept their secret: both were members of the IRA, who at this time were wreaking havoc in Britain in support of the Irish cause. They were men trained to build and utilise improvised explosive devices (IEDs) to kill and maim in support of their country. It was a dangerous game, they knew that someday it would inevitably affect the innocent but they were recruited under oath to fight the British and to do what was needed it required total allegiance to the cause.

Barney Coughlin was born and bred in County Down, Northern Ireland. Trained as a motor mechanic, and later becoming disillusioned with ordinary life, he yearned for excitement, and to get it he and Declan joined the Irish Republican Army. They dreamt of fame and legend, of being remembered as rebel heroes, their names carved in stone

He was chosen and trained by the IRA in most aspects of guerrilla warfare. At first he worked diligently with a strong belief in what he was doing, but as reality crept in he became more aware of the distinct possibility of hurting or maiming others; it was Catholic upbringing and strict family ethics that gave him a problem, and his dedication to the cause was slowly diminishing.

It wasn't long before he was suffering from depression, and it was time to make a very serious but difficult decision; that is, to break the pledge. He knew doing so would bring pain and heartache to himself and others, and the hardest thing would be the subsequent rift between him and his friends and family.

He had taken the oath shortly after joining the IRA, and in the early stages of his new role, life was pleasant. He made good friends, and other than the hard training he was beginning to get the best from his new and different lifestyle. He was looking forward to the future.

After his training, once he was passed out, his commanders did not wait long before Barney and Declan were assigned their first job. They were transferred to Shetland, and at first their new role was strange to them, but life on site continued to be good, and it wasn't long before the mood changed and things started to get serious: their first target, once confirmed, was much bigger than he had ever imagined; the consequences enormous.

Declan and Barney had dreamt of becoming heroes, worshipped by all Irish nationalists fighting the cause, but what the two expected in their dreams was different than the real thing. The prevailing situation had become serious and they soon realised that if they were successful in what they were planning would surely impact the stability of Europe.

The Shetland Mainland and the surrounding islands are positioned approximately two hundred miles to the north of Scotland. The weather there is inclement most of the time, and during the winter months it can be an intolerable place to work. The wind blows incessantly; this makes life difficult for the construction industry, in which heavy lifting is usually necessary.

The completion of construction work on the Terminal had a forecast date for May 1981 and in this highly competitive European market, this date was important; it would bring stability, prestige and confidence to the UK economy.

So important was this event to the UK that HM Queen Elizabeth, Prince Phillip and King Olav of Norway were all scheduled to attend the opening ceremony.

Barney and Declan were now part of a terrorist army, and their orders were to assassinate all on the platform at the opening, a task that exceeded everything they had dared to imagine.

This challenge was bigger than anything previously carried out by the IRA and the team assigned to do it were two virtually inexperienced agents led by a deranged Irish academic.

Nevertheless the Irish Commander directing operations from his Dublin base believed the three were a very good team and would carry out their task effectively.

The leader of this Republican group was a man called Michael O'Byrne, and soon after he joined the IRA the KGB also recruited him. However, his reign was not to last long as British Intelligence at Glasgow Airport detained him on his first flight to the Shetland!

As the date of the big event drew ever closer, Barney became more nervous. He started to lose sleep, thought continually of the folk that might get hurt, and the risk to the young and innocent who could be caught in the crossfire.

The moment of truth came in August 1979 with the assassination of Lord Mountbatten, who was killed on a boat whilst on holiday with friends on the west coast of Ireland.

There were other people on the boat that were also killed including his grandson and a young local boat boy.

On the same day, at a place called Narrow Water Castle close to the town of Warrenpoint, seventeen British soldiers were also assassinated.

Barney started to have second thoughts. How would the relatives – the mothers, fathers, brothers, sisters, and friends of the slain – cope with their unexpected loss, this waste of human life? He broke down; he did not agree with the violence that the nationalists had adopted against the British; it would he thought bring even more death and destruction in each assault. He felt uncomfortable regarding his position and felt he may need to abscond from this work. Such an action is not easy, no matter what the circumstances. The seriousness of breaking his oath to the Republican army and shattering his boyhood dream, but it was a matter of having faith in himself before it was too late; the consequences he knew were unforgivable for his comrades, the members of the IRA who had been fighting for their cause for many years. He believed in the diplomatic freedom that the nationalists were striving to achieve and the cause that had vowed allegiance, but he could never understand the British Parliament's obstinacy in not coming to an agreement. With such dreadful hostilities, there is almost certainly death; there will be injury and hate, bitterness will grow in the minds of all involved, and the deaths of people is inevitable. A terrorist's mind is normally radicalised; their methods, if carried out intensively, will be unfaltering; they will stand by the rules, obey to the nth degree and if necessary die for the cause.

During his training, as Barney listened to his IRA tutors, at the time he thought he understood the principles they taught him, but he did not consider what was really expected of him; that is, to carry out instructions and never consider the consequences.

When he was recruited he was young and strong, and felt he could overcome anything and feel nothing. He was wrong – those talks of bravado that he spent hours talking with his friend Declan were now, he felt, incorrect and it was clear that they now had different opinions: Declan to fight on and Barney to opt for a life of peace, he was after all just a simple boy from the country.

Now he was on the run as a fugitive, his main concern was not to get killed, and to remain free and hopefully find a place to live in peace. A traitor, yes; he now needed to redeem his integrity and to help others, especially those who couldn't help themselves.

He was now compassionate, and no longer a terrorist.

LIVING ROUGH

It was getting late and Barney decided to keep out of sight and sleep rough for the night. He was lucky enough to pass a newsagent and stole old newspapers from the rack outside the shop. This was to pack inside his clothes to keep out the cold whilst he slept.

The next morning, he rose from his bed feeling cold and miserable. His muscles were stiff, his bones ached; he needed to move. He forced himself to run as fast as he could manage and getting out of breath slowed to a jog and then started to walk, the warmth from the exercise returning to his body.

It was still early as he ambled through the streets and came across a railway station. It was Fenchurch Street, and checking his money purchased a ticket to the end of the line on the first train to depart.

An hour later he disembarked at Tilbury Docks and hailed a taxi and asked the driver to take him somewhere close that had accommodation to rent, the cheaper and more isolated the better. "He was after peace," he said.

2

AFTER HIBERNATION, MARCH 1981

It was the last Sunday in March, the first time he had ventured out since his walk in London.

It was important that he kept himself private, alone and away from the bustling crowds, and during the last six months he had tried to maintain a monastic life, but now it was necessary to face the world and escape from this dark hole in the middle of nowhere. He felt after the first few months that insanity was close; it seemed a long time since the taxi had dropped him off at the farm, in fact it seemed an eternity. He had to get out and face the world.

The rooms where he had lived were dark, cold and damp. He had expected them to be bad, as this was made clear to him when he agreed terms with the old farmer who owned them, but he could never have imagined at that time just how uninhabitable the place would prove to be. He paid the rent for half the year in advance with cash. No agent, no other fees, the price and terms were good, the area quiet, no interaction with anybody except the staff in the local corner store, and he managed to maintain his obscurity. But his mental state had begun to suffer; he needed to mingle, to read the newspapers, to see how people were living in the real world.

Many nights in this damp, dark place had played with his mind; in his dreams his ageing mother had come to him and tried to convince him that arrest and imprisonment would be a better option than running away; that in prison he could at least have a warm shower, eat well and have visits from loved ones.

He soon realised that his mind had gone astray; he needed to be positive, and move on.

A new identity would give him a gateway to another world, a world without hate and terror, and another chance. It might never be a reality, trying to achieve the improbable, perhaps even the impossible dream.

His nightmares continued to keep him awake; he was convinced that if the IRA got to him first it would be summary execution. He wondered whether jail might well be the better option. He shivered; if caught by the police, he would live, but it would be many years before he got out of prison – he would go mad.

If a reversal of his situation were possible, what he would give to return to his beautiful village that nestled at the foot of the Mourne Mountains! In the unlikely event he did return home he would face personal humiliation, disgrace for his family, being branded as a coward – the easiest way out could be a bullet. Who would find him first?

He shuddered, steadied himself and slumped down on the nearest bench. It was close to the river, a spot for relaxation. He scanned the map of London and tried to visualise the best area to find a 'home'.

MAKING A DECISION TO LIVE

He returned to Tilbury and, later that evening whilst in his room, decided to make a break for the Big Smoke as early as possible. Before retiring he packed a small haversack with essentials, tidied the room and jumped into bed.

He was awakened early the next morning by a tractor starting up outside; he got up and prepared for his trip to the city.

Barney had anticipated that he would leave the rooms when the six months was up, and had informed the farmer that this would be the case. All rent was paid with a week in hand.

It was a long walk to the nearest railway station but he thought it better to walk than to trust a taxi. He started early and by 10.30 boarded the train at Grays Railway Station. It was bound for London Fenchurch Street; a return to where he had come from. The carriage was empty, but it was warm and comfortable, so he sat down and soon was immersed in a magazine he found tucked between the seats. It was a dubious read; turning the first shining page he found a full-frontal nude photograph of Brigitte Bardot. Other parts of the magazine were filled with nude females in various lurid positions, and he became intoxicated, a young man high on testosterone.

The train trundled along and shuddered to a stop at the first few stations. Nobody entered his compartment and it seemed quiet, which suited his mood.

But he was soon disappointed when the train halted at Barking and suddenly pandemonium reigned; hordes of young people boarded and jammed into the carriage, and in a second it changed from total peace to mayhem.

Trying to remain inconspicuous, Barney kept his head down and scanned the magazine. It was not long before the girl who had squeezed in next to him looked over his shoulder, and what she read made her laugh. Quite to his horror, she shared what she had seen in the magazine with the rest of the carriage. The others found it a great joke, and their conversation turned to Barney. He was suddenly a prominent and not the solitary figure he wanted – to them it was a joke; to him it was a total embarrassment. Caught out and humiliated, he held his head low, avoiding eye contact and wishing that they all would go away and leave him to be alone.

But soon Barney went from being embarrassed to being angry; he realised that by attracting so much attention, he may have blown his cover, and could easily have been exposed due to his own stupidity. He jammed the magazine into the gap between the seats as he had found it, and turned to stare out of the window.

"Do you mind?" said the girl next to him, retrieving the magazine, and with a smile on her face she passed it around the carriage. It seemed to be the centre of attention for the next twenty minutes before the train finally pulled into Fenchurch Street Station.

"Good on you, mate," some of the young Londoners shouted back across the carriage as they disembarked, thinking it a great joke, and elevating Barney, he felt, to a mini 'train carriage hero'.

"Great show, old man," said another, holding his thumb high to Barney as he skirted down the station platform, and as quickly as they arrived, so they were gone; the carriage was again peaceful, the only noise coming from the bustling main-line station outside.

By creating such a stir, he had brought undue attention to himself; it was a mistake, totally unprofessional. Although the youngsters had been enjoying themselves and it was an innocent tease, luckily not detrimental to his security, he was learning quickly that this situation must never happen again.

Leaving the station and his shame behind him, he walked aimlessly along the busy London streets. After about a mile he checked his map, and stubbed his forefinger on the place where he now stood: Threadneedle Street. He ran his finger along the co-ordinate where the road headed in the direction of London Bridge, and walked in that direction; then he turned right and headed for St Paul's. With the huge cathedral on his right, he turned left, heading downhill to Blackfriars Bridge, and crossed the river on the footbridge. It was on the other side that he began to feel tired; it was rest he needed, but where was he going? Where would he spend the night? He was confused, and once again sat down on a nearby bench. From the map and the position between the bridges he guessed he was close to Shakespeare's rebuilt Globe Theatre; once this was established he collected his thoughts regarding his strategy for a night on the tiles.

He had been on the run for a total of nine months, since that day he made the decision to quit his job and turn his back on the IRA. It was a long time for a traitor to be on the run!

3

LOOKING FOR A LIFE, MAY 1981

It was a bright day in early May, and a cool breeze was blowing from the north but the wind direction suddenly changed to a south-easterly direction bringing with it a warmer temperature that was a pleasant relief.

Barney felt frustrated – he did not look forward to sleeping on the streets, but it was anywhere he could find that might be suitable for a fugitive; he sought privacy and safety in a London that was so busy.

His last accommodation, which was that wretched place near Tilbury, was now behind him, and he was happy to be away from it, having spent the last six months in a place that he despised. This great city had things to offer, an underworld where anything could be bought; this was the best place, outside of Belfast, his nearest city. London was a place full of opportunities, but only if he knew the right places to go to get what he wanted.

He needed to get away from England, to find a place to hide where his pursuers could not find him; it was an impending priority.

Having saved money from his time working in Shetland, part of this was now stashed in a safe deposit box in Glasgow, a small amount carried inside his shoes, and the remainder buried in a safe place; at least that is what he hoped. He was far from being penniless, but without earning he would need to be careful.

The task of establishing a new identity was now crucial for him to survive; he would require a passport and a National Health number. Other essentials included a birth certificate, appropriate parental names, a medical and educational history, household bills – the list seemed endless, so he would need to get busy, but how, and what illegalities he would need to commit to achieve this, was another thing!

Whilst training with the IRA he had studied the methods that his sponsors used to create false identities. These were now to provide him with the ideas and opportunities to do it.

The positive thoughts he was having as he strolled along the Embankment made him happy. It gave him a spring in his step, and he felt content as he crossed at London Bridge and headed towards Aldgate and onto the Commercial Road, but as the hours passed the walking had now made him tired in both body and mind and all he now wanted was to sleep, but where to find a place to bed down in this old city, a lonely place for a fugitive?

Turning down a backstreet adjacent to a flyover, the area seemed shabby and he thought he might get advice from the homeless who lived here. Passing the flyover arches, he noticed a group of what looked like homeless people in conversation. A muscled male was doing most of the talking, his bare chest exposed to the chill air, but the cold did not seem to bother him. Two others, their gender unclear, sat up, half covered with a duvet, whilst another male, also well muscled, stood paring a piece of wood with a short knife, his long red hair in locks that flowed down his back. He was a big man standing well over six feet tall, his tanned skin a backdrop to his many fading tattoos.

Barney was apprehensive and reached into his pockets, searching for some coins he could offer them.

The man with the knife turned to talk with the others, but then noticed Barney walking towards them and immediately stiffened and fixed his eyes suspiciously in his direction. "Look up, could be the Old Bill," laughed the man, his stare directed at the newcomer. With his long red hair swirling in the cool breeze, he pocketed the knife, moved forward a few steps, and blocked Barney's path. "What have we here, my trendy friend?" The red-headed man was imposing, and with hands on hips glared at his pending prey.

Barney stopped, withdrew his hand from his pocket and offered the coins to his antagonist.

"It's not coins I want, smarty; they'll not keep the weather out. It's your coat I fancy; that will keep me warm." He was aggressive, snarling as he spoke.

Barney put the money back into his pocket and, sensing trouble, let his arms dangle by his sides, awaiting the man's next move. They stared hard at each other, Barney taking the first incentive.

"My name is Barney Coughlin..." His voice tailed off, and he thought quickly – that should not have been said. Now completely flustered, he stammered, searching his mind for a pseudonym. "It's John Brightling..." His tone of voice did not sound convincing.

"You lying little toad." The big man grabbed Barney around his throat and smashed a fist into his face.

"Fuck you, you son of a bitch!" Smarting from the blow, his left eye already swelling, Barney backed off and circled the redhead, trying to clear his head, not knowing whether to turn and run or stay and fight. The latter was surely coming.

Another man joined them, smaller but agile-looking. Barney had heard them talking earlier; his name was Falcon. Even with a fast-swelling left eye he feared the worst – hanging from Falcon's hand was a club about a metre in length and about thirty centimetres in girth at the top end; an ugly and dangerous-looking weapon.

Barney tried to concentrate; he was frightened, but in a position of no return. The tall red-headed man made his move, his huge fists about to be unleashed on the Irishman, who tried to think of his old boxing moves. They felt a million miles away but he followed his instinct and moved in a circular fashion away from the right side of his opponent, hoping that he might nullify the attacks using his left fist or foot.

His old fighting instinct suddenly took over and he moved quickly towards the redhead, catching him off balance. He hit the man with three quick punches and moved back out of his reach, becoming more confident that his talent had not deserted him.

But it was the two assailants working in tandem that proved to be a problem for Barney, and at the very last moment the man with the club joined the action and swung it ferociously at Barney's face. He swayed out of reach, the club missing his head by a few inches. Barney again moved deftly forward, but the club came round again and this time hit him in the ribs, winding him. He staggered back, trying to breath. Redhead and Falcon then descended upon the backtracking fugitive, and this time the club struck him on the knee, felling the Irishman in an instant.

Barney lay still on the ground, and as Falcon raised the club for another onslaught, Redhead held him back. "That's enough; you may kill him. It won't be much of a loss but the Old Bill will never let us alone."

Falcon ignored the bigger man and moved forward with the club held high, and again his friend held him back again.

"Enough, Falcon!" Redhead shouted. "I said that's enough. Cool it, man." He paused before adding, "All I want is his coat, and I am sure he will give it up easily now."

Falcon seemed agitated. "What about me? I want something from this too." He seemed indignant that Redhead had not included him in the spoils of war.

"Ask him what else he can offer, and I am sure it will not be a problem, will it, Boxer Boy?"

Falcon looked down at the defeated Irishman. Barney was squirming on the floor, grimacing with pain.

"Well, stranger, the coat, please, and make it a friendly gesture; you may need to talk with my, er, colleague regarding a further settlement before he knocks your brains out," Redhead snarled at Barney. He kicked over a small fruit box. "Sit down, if you want, but take the coat off first." Redhead scowled.

Barney removed his coat, and slowly and painfully sat down on the broken fruit box, a remnant of the local market. He attempted to pull his thoughts together, to think of something that would appease Falcon; he had had enough action for one day.

Redhead was not happy; the coat was far too small for his muscular body, and it felt like a straitjacket. "Bloody thing is too tight," he moaned.

"I have very little to give you, and all I came here for was to find out how I can live like you do, because I have nothing and no place to go." Barney, looking for sympathy, paused and just stared at the ground. "I have little money; probably not enough to buy something warm to sleep in tonight," he lied again.

"You don't look like a down-and-out: nice clothes, shaven and showered – what are you talking about?" scoffed Redhead.

"I got sacked, caught stealing from the safe, then hit the security officer before fleeing to the country," Barney lied. "This happened in Ireland, where I come from."

Redhead took off Barney's coat and laid it on the ground. "Maybe it will suit Falcon more than me."

Falcon came back and Redhead filled him in on the situation.

"How much have you got?" He nodded to Barney.

"Thirty pounds."

"Then I can fix you up with a duvet and waterproof, for fifty. I'll take the thirty now and collect the rest later – take it or leave it!" sneered Falcon.

"That leaves me skint."

"And that will not be the last time. When will you start to sleep in the duvet?"

"Tonight."

"OK, I will bring it here in an hour."

Barney at first found the night cold, but soon he realised that his newly acquired duvet was paying dividends. He was soon warm, and found comfort in the few fellow dwellers also tucked up in similar bedding, most of it having seen better days.

Falcon wandered over to him as if to have a chat, but the beaten Irishman, sensing his movements, closed his eyes and pretended to be asleep.

Falcon stood over the slumbering Irishman. "Goodnight, Irish; remember you still owe me – another twenty, and we want it tomorrow. If we don't get it, watch your arse, 'cause we will really finish the job."

His newly acquired coat looked impeccable as he turned away and disappeared into the streets.

Barney felt resentful. He wanted to find a way to get even; not necessarily a fight, but a way that would hurt them. If it was to happen it must not draw attention to himself.

With his blood pumping and temper high, he wanted retribution, but thinking of a way to do the job this could be counterproductive to his goal. Maybe later – this was not the time, and despite his agitation fatigue took over and he fell into a deep sleep.

4

CHARLES'S WIFE,
APRIL 1981

Barney woke just after dawn and, not wanting to encounter his antagonists from the previous day, decided to get out and walk. Moving briskly, his heart began to pound, and with his mind cleared, he focused on the real problem: a new identity. Without it he would be static and sooner or later arrested, so now was the time to make his first move and make contact with the right people who would arrange it.

During his training period Barney had learnt the methods by which the IRA obtained new identities: either by cloning a living person's details or by utilising information taken from a dead person. When cloning or stealing a living person's private information, he was aware, computers could discover any duplication quickly, so the potential imposter should ensure that identical names were not on the local register. He thought it may be a better choice to search the national; it could be less detectable.

It was obvious to Barney that the dead-person option was the way to go. Although in this case a deeper search for details was necessary, the information required could be found more readily from local infantile knowledge. This could include working back from the gravestones of young people who had recently died, ascertaining who their parents were and where they lived. Checks on the dead person's National Insurance number, passport and accounts would provide all that was required to create the traceability necessary.

Now totally paranoid, and confused, he needed direction; someone who knew how to live illegally, forge documents or tell him how to do it.

He continued to hypothesise, walking aimlessly along narrow streets, the houses small and terraced, before reaching a busy crossroads and a small shop-cum-café.

"A coffee, please," he asked the Indian owner.

"What type do you want? Americano, café con leche, latte? Please choose and sit down; I will bring to you."

Barney was astounded at the choices available.

"Just a strong coffee with milk, please."

In a few minutes, Barney received his coffee. It lifted him and he felt upbeat, positive – why this sudden uplift? He thought it was the caffeine, or perhaps the fresh air? Whatever it was, he was feeling good.

His mind now very active, one side of it was telling him to be aggressive, to make things happen, to be driven; but his quieter side was telling him to be patient, and keep his eyes and ears to the ground in an attempt to locate a person who could produce the new identity he so desperately wanted.

His first priority was to retrieve his worldly belongings from where he had slept the previous night and then make a break for it, before his predators returned. Redhead and Falcon would need to wait for their money, and Barney was still sore from the beating he'd taken the night before; his body and legs ached, and his face had blackened as the bruises surfaced on his skin. In pain, he returned to where his belongings had been left earlier.

Immediately as he turned into the road where his bedding was stored, his heart skipped a beat. Directly ahead and coming his way were Red and Falcon.

He thought it might be best to cross the road, but then thought this too obvious; they would meet him halfway and all hell would let loose.

They were within ten yards of him when Falcon stepped out into the road. Big Red quickened, moving directly towards Barney; he knew there would be no words, only blows. They wanted the rest of their money, but as bruised as he was, this time he felt it would be different; his temper was rising, and when Falcon was within range, he skipped to his left and threw a left hook. Immediately ducking low for more leverage, he followed up with a crashing right hook to Falcon's stomach; he heard him gasp, but before he could adjust his position to tackle Red, the big man was on him, grabbing his hair and slamming his own forehead against Barney's. The crack of skull hitting skull sounded like a branch breaking from a tree.

Falcon quickly recovered, mainly due to his new coat that cushioned the Irishman's blow. As Red surged forward towards Barney, Falcon dropped onto one knee and grasped Barney by the ankle. Now off balance, the Irishman fell to the ground.

It was useless; the feeling in his legs had gone and Big Red took advantage. He hit Barney on the side of his face, and he groaned, although, despite being in a semi-conscious state, remained in a sitting position. Big Red stood tall, and started to remove his belt. But as he did so, a scream made both predators freeze.

They looked to see where the sound came from and saw a woman standing only twenty yards away at the corner of the street.

"Get off that man; stop it! I have phoned the police; they will be here in less than two minutes." She waved her hands in the air demonstrating her alleged call.

"Fuck the slag," said Red, "let's go," and Falcon followed as he disappeared down a side road.

The woman ran to Barney, who was trying unsuccessfully to stand.

"Don't move." She held him down.

He gritted his teeth. "Have you called the police?" he gasped, still in pain.

"Don't be silly, dear boy; if I did that I would have nobody to help, would I?"

From her bag she brought out various medical supplies that she used to clean up Barney.

"I can do nothing for the bruises, they need a cold compress, but I don't think that anything is broken, so if you can walk we can get out of here before they return. Those two look like a mean couple of individuals."

It was still early in the morning and, apart from a few homeless individuals hanging about, little was going on. It seemed that nobody else in the vicinity cared about the skirmish, or for that matter who had been involved.

"My name is Sarah," the woman said.

"And mine is Barney – sorry, no, it is Brightling," Barney stammered.

"Now, now, I need to call you something and the truth would be the best place to start." She was firm.

"At home it is Barney, but here on the streets, I call myself Brightling." He paused for a moment, thinking about what he had said to this lady. She was a total stranger.

"We need to get you to a safe place away from this rumpus; it will be better for you to stay in my flat until you feel better, then you must go elsewhere." She was excited from the confrontation with Red and Falcon and she was breathing hard as she spoke.

"Why are you doing this?" Barney asked.

"Doing what?"

"Saving me from another beating, and now taking me home." He was surprised.

"Because I am a Samaritan helping the poor and needy."
She started to help him to his feet. "I live in a small mews flat-cum-house behind Parade Street, close to Paddington Station. You may stay there until you are well; then you must move on." Her tone was serious and to the point.

Once he was standing, and after he had retrieved his bedding, she hailed a taxi.

Twenty-five minutes later Barney found himself in a very comfortable mews home, a small building built originally as an annex for the main house. Since the nineteenth century the rich owners had been hit by two world wars, their fortunes had dwindled and the main part of the houses had been split into affordable dwellings and sold to the highest bidders. Before this hardship had hit the financially better-off people in London they lived on different floors to their staff. The large houses in London also included a small house built in the garden to accommodate the gardeners and their peacocks, the latter used to scare away intruders; thus the name 'mews'. With accommodation at a premium early in the twentieth century, these small dwellings were converted into individual households, one of which was now Sarah's home.

She helped Barney climb the stairs to her front door, guiding him through the flat into the spare bedroom. On reaching the side of the bed he immediately collapsed onto it and closed his eyes.

"Stay there until you feel better and I will make you a cup of tea and help you into some different clothes."

"Thank you, ma'am. I will be up and about tomorrow."

"I doubt it, but we will see." She left the room and headed towards the kitchen.

It was about ten minutes later when she returned with a pot of tea, a shirt and some joggers.

"Get yourself into these, my good man, and we will see how you are tomorrow. If you stay longer, the neighbours will talk. So what is your name?"

" Brightling."

"Your real name please, mister – didn't you say it was Barney?"

"OK, ma'am, it is Barney." He felt bad about lying to Sarah; she had rescued him from a severe beating after all.

"OK, Barney, you will tell me the whole truth, not the lies, please."

He held back his reply as she had left the room to get her own cup of coffee.

She returned to his room stirring the coffee, and sat down on a chair at the end of his bed.

"Now, you cannot stay here another day until you tell me your story – no lies, please, only the truth."

She stared at him; her head bent at thirty degrees, her eyes glaring. He turned his head away, not knowing what to say.

"I am waiting." It was an instruction.

He was sworn to secrecy, and he was biding his time. Without a reply she arose from the chair and left the room, cup still in hand. He fell into a deep sleep on top of the bed.

Sarah was very athletic and looked younger then her fifty-three years, she seemed pleased with herself as she looked at herself in the mirror before donning a light coat and slipping out onto the iron exit stairway and headed for Paddington Tube Station; she had a lunch date with her lady friends.

She was late arriving, and offered profuse apologies upon seeing them, but did not respond to their jokes, which all seemed to harp on the 'man in your flat' theme. They were teasing her in the event she was never late for their gatherings. After some further bantering they all settled down to lunch and the piffle that elderly women base their discussions on. Anyone outside the group would have thought they had not seen each other for years, not that it had been just a week since they had met previously.

Cynthia, who seemed to be the leader of the group, latched on to Sarah's predicament and turned to the late arrival. "So, Sarah, today you are so quiet, very unnatural for you, and you seem to be in a dream. Are you missing Charles, or is there something else you need to share?"

"Sorry to disappoint you, dear Cynthia, but life is still very boring without my dear Charles, nevertheless I must go early today, I have a parcel to collect at the post office."

After apologies Sarah left lunch feeling somewhat agitated regarding the conversation that she thought intruding.

She decided to walk back to Paddington along the Marylebone Road; she aimlessly perused every shop that she passed, not seeing anything but thinking about her situation.

Her husband Charles had died some nine months previously. She was still in mourning and lonely, and until Barney had come along she'd had nobody to share her life with.

Her intention after her loss had been to keep mind and body busy. She joined a charity to aid the homeless and her life began to brighten; she met other people, kept herself busy – the intent was that she would be tired at the end of the day and ready for nothing but sleep.

The situation with Barney did change things; she had not expected to get caught up in a street fight, take in the vanquished and shoulder his troubles as well as her own. She secretly hoped that his story would be interesting but innocent once she got it out of him, and that those dreadful men had taken liberties with a gentleman.

Since Charles had passed she had become nervous of men, keeping them at a distance, but then out of the blue came this handsome young bull of a man to complicate her life. At fifty-three years old she was no young woman, yet his very presence made her ache with longing. She did not know if it was desire or her mothering instinct to hold the young man as the child she never had. She longed to be touched, to be wanted, to act without conscience in bed.

Her own thoughts excited her; she stumbled whilst crossing the road under the Marylebone Flyover and stopped upon reaching a path; a precautionary effort to stop herself falling. She was now close to home, she needed to pull herself together, but she felt powerless against him. What if he made advances? She would be defenceless, no resistance; it would be a disaster, a mistake.

She turned into Paddington Station and stopped for a coffee. She faltered as she checked the menu, decided on a caffè latte but changed it to a cappuccino, then sat down and intended to make it last as long as possible.

"Hello?" she called on entering the flat.

His reply came from the kitchen. "Apologies, but I slept and missed you." He seemed concerned by her absence.

"Oh, I had a lunch date with some female friends," she said, looking out of the window.

"How was it?"

"It was OK; we meet once a week." She turned away towards the lounge. "If you are to stay for a few days I need my questions answered."

"Of course, I must apologise again, it seems to be becoming a habit, but my name is..." He fell silent for a few seconds before shaking his head.

"Your name is...?" Her eyes narrowed as she glanced in his direction, and she continued talking. "Please do not insult me by falsifying everything; the last thing I want is a trail of lies."

"I cannot tell you everything but what I do tell you will be the truth, and if that is not good enough I understand and will make alternative arrangements. My humble thanks, ma'am, for all you have done." He picked up his coat and turned to leave.

She held herself back, wanting to rush and stop him, then spoke to him gently. "If you are interested, I can hold a secret and will do so if you so wish; nevertheless, it would be good manners on your part if you told me your real name."

She did not want to be in the house alone; she wanted him to stay. She sensed he was of a gentle nature and was intent on finding out his story. "Come, sit down. I will make a cup of tea and you can tell me your story – that is, the bits you're allowed to tell me!"

He so wanted to tell someone, to clear his mind; if not a priest in confession, then it would have to be with Sarah.

5

CONFESSIONS WITHIN

Sarah sat expectant; she needed to know who this man in her house was, this person who was emotionally tormenting her. Silently, she waited. The minutes ticked by, they could have been hours, but, remaining patient, she just gazed at the floor.

Barney cleared his throat. "I was born in a village in Northern Ireland, a beautiful place called Rostrevor, close to Carlingford Lough. The banks are lined with redwood trees that grow tall and elegant and sway with the breeze from the lough. Its location is close to the border between the north of Ireland and the south; the scent of danger from terrorists is ever present.

He went on. "I have a close friend; his name is Declan. We shared a strong nationalistic political view but the British – and the prevailing situation – stirred instincts within so we decided to do our duty and join the Irish Republican Army. It was not the nationalistic side of it so much as the excitement that we craved; you must understand that Declan and I were the only two left of our childhood friends as all had moved away to pastures new."

He paused between breaths, but Sarah interrupted, "Why did you—"

He ignored her as though in a trance. "I was trained as a bomb technician and Declan and I were assigned to Sullom Voe in Shetland, a huge oil and gas terminal that was in the process of construction. Our task was to set an IED at the opening ceremony. I hate to mention the important people that would be affected." He looked up at her to see her response.

"My God," exclaimed Sarah. "What happened? Who were these people?"

"Those intending to be on the platform were no less than the British Queen, her husband Philip, and King Olav of Norway."

"My goodness, this gets worse." Sarah was aghast.

"I lived on the camp at Sullom Voe for many months working for a building contractor, and during my spare time assembled and tested many IEDs, but my mind played games with me. It was only after the assassination of Lord Mountbatten and his entourage at Sligo in August '79, and on the same day seventeen young British soldiers were assassinated near Warrenpoint, that I realised that the life was not for me."

"What happened? Has the terminal been opened?" gasped Sarah.

"It should have been opened by now, but I have not kept up with the news at all during the last few months." He did not know the current situation nor any of the activities that had gone on since his departure, and he lied to her now, because if the operation went ahead and was thwarted he would be worse than a liar.

She stared at him with disbelief. "What will you do? Are the police hunting you? There are so many questions…" She was beside herself.

"It seems that the IRA, MI5, MI6, the Ulster Constabulary and the British police all want to question me," he felt deflated as he guessed at the situation.

"But why are they after you? Do they know that you were not involved when you left, or did you tell them?" Sarah felt the need to know more.

"It appears there was a tip-off resulting in some arrests but I do not know much about that as I wasn't there."

Sarah continued her aggressive questioning. "Who were you responsible to?"

He looked at her directly, his face serious. "I stop at this, ma'am. I think for your own good that enough has been said."

Sarah could not believe the story and sat on the sofa, her eyes wild. It suddenly dawned on her that she was harbouring an IRA fugitive. Her mind was in turmoil; she could take no more.

"Goodnight, Barney. You've left me with much to think about, but we will talk again soon." And with that she slowly walked to her bedroom, closing the door quietly as she did so.

Sarah Siddons was born in Yorkshire and came from a wealthy farming family. After five years at university, first studying medicine, then dropping out to study politics, she joined the British Army where she became a trained nurse and rose up to matron and held the rank of first lieutenant. There she met her husband Charles, whilst he was recovering from a bomb blast in Belfast; so after he was medically discharged they lived in Hereford, where she worked in the local hospital and had in recent years acted as matron.

The explosion had left Charles with post-traumatic stress disorder and it was necessary for her to retire and nurse him until he mysteriously disappeared just under a year ago.

Since his apparent death she had become desperately lonely, and decided to join a charity organisation for the homeless and help with their problems. Little did she think that her life would change so much in just a few days.

Now she had befriended a man over twenty years younger than her, a member of the IRA: she had become reckless, blinded by circumstances. Realisation dawned: was she now culpable by association?

It was absurd and she tried to dismiss it from her mind – it would only bring embarrassment and heartache; it was no means to an end.

Perhaps it was the physical aspect: the femininity within her needed him around. It gave her more vitality – she no longer had the looks and skin of a twenty-year-old, but he made her feel younger, gave her a reason to live. At night she was restless, sleepless, trying to justify her amicability towards him. He was a wanted man, sought by the police, and she was guilty by association.

Feeling particularly restless one night, she rose, unhooked her gown from the wardrobe door, and scurried off to the kitchen for a glass of milk. Clearing the small corridor from the bedroom, she brushed through the lounge, it was without light, and, on entering the kitchen, poured herself a large glass of milk. After drinking it slowly, she felt better; the cool, smooth liquid seemed to settle her stomach and she turned back towards her bedroom.

As she backtracked through the lounge, she was astounded to see Barney slumped on the armchair in the corner of the room reading by torchlight. He was totally unaware of her.

"Barney, you must rest and build up as much strength as possible; you can only stay a short while longer." She stood above him, holding her glass; she was dictating to him, an instruction that she was convinced was not what she really wanted.

Barney smiled and shot a glance at Sarah. "Thank you, Sarah; I know that. You have been good to me, and don't worry – I am OK and will move on shortly!"

She felt guilty for her harsh comments, and moved around to face him and apologise rather than talk to him over his shoulder. As she moved stealthily around the armchair her robe caught on the arm; it became loose and, anticipating a disaster, she quickly sat down on the arm to keep her gown from opening fully. But this made things worse: the arm was narrower than she thought and she lost her balance, falling onto the unprepared Barney. The weight of both of them tipped the armchair and turned it over on its side, spilling them onto the floor. The robe, still snagged on the arm, was pulled from her body, and she was left naked, perilously close to the unsuspecting Irishman.

Just for a moment in the turmoil he remained inert, stunned first by the accident, then the embarrassment of being so close to her naked body.

"Oh! Oh! I am so sorry, Barney." She scrambled to free herself from his arms, but his hands were holding her; he felt aroused. She attempted to scramble free, but in an instant their faces were almost touching. It was enough: fuelled with passion, they spontaneously kissed; her instincts got the better of her and she wildly pulled the buttons from his shirt. He spread his hands over her body; the thirty years' difference in age was irrelevant.

It was daylight when Barney stirred, his naked body lying close to the sleeping Sarah. Her face looked content, her body curled towards him; she looked to him quite beautiful sleeping peacefully on her side. Quietly he rose from the floor, straightened the upturned chair and, collecting his clothes from where they were strewn, made his way to his bedroom, collapsed on the unmade bed and again fell asleep.

Two weeks had now passed and Barney was keeping his head down, going out for a walk only at night.

Sarah had now accepted his situation, totally convinced that he was an honest but misguided man, one who had turned away from evil, away from hurting others. She was content for him to stay; she had no guilt or concern regarding the neighbours or what her friends thought of her situation, swallowing her pride in the process.

They had only slept together twice, and both times the act had been tender but simple, she not wanting to show her long marriage experience to the younger man too readily, but there was time and she longed for him to stay.

Barney felt guilty regarding his deceit, but he was driven towards another life, ever thoughtful, his mind forever scheming. Life would never be quite the same for him as in those carefree days in Rostrevor; he yearned for his freedom and autonomy, a new identity, a new life.

During his stay with Sarah his plans were progressing better than he had ever imagined. He now had to find a way to put things into perspective and cover his escape plan once it was initiated.

Sarah confided in him, and discussed the circumstances of her husband's death. The controversial issue, she explained, was that there was no conclusive evidence; his body had never been found.

His clothing was discovered on a beach in Devon early one morning during their holiday. He had apparently gone for his early-morning swim but had not returned to the hotel. A sea search followed without success, and he was listed as 'missing, presumed dead'. During the enquiry his army record and disability were taken into account and the case was left open by the coroner. She mentioned that during the months since his death their business interests had remained the same; she had not closed his accounts or his credit cards.

Barney took every opportunity to explore the flat when Sarah was not there, and his dishonesty started to pay dividends. He discovered Charles's passport, his National Insurance number, receipts and household bills; he familiarised himself with information gained from Charles's business diary, and took notes of his medical history.

Armed with this information, he applied for a new passport. It was fortunate that the two men were similar in looks and physique; the difference in age was not obvious in Charles's passport photograph and when it was necessary he would make up his face to suit the picture in the passport.

Once he had received his new identity, his name would change forever to Charles Siddons. This was something that he could not face with Sarah – she would not accept this situation, and nor would Barney want her to!

6

A SIMPLE LIFE

Naomi Zimba was born in Johannesburg in 1953. Her father was called Chaka, and he was named after the famous Zulu chieftain. Her mother Hilda was also Zulu, born and bred in a small village close to the town of Lundazi in the eastern province of Zambia. She was from the same village as her future husband, though the two did not forge a friendship until later.

Searching for a better life, Hilda had moved to Johannesburg after her twenty-sixth birthday in 1946 and met Chaka at an ANC rally a few months later. After a year they married and both found jobs in Johannesburg, Hilda in service and Chaka as a gardener.

Hilda was of mixed race; her biological father was an Scottish farmer called Peterson, and her mother, a maid, worked on his farm. It was not uncommon in the early days of Dutch settlement for associations to happen in this way, and Hilda's mother Beatrice often explained her side of the story in vivid detail whenever the subject arose.

The association between Beatrice and Peterson turned out well for her, as the old farmer bequeathed a sizeable legacy to his mistress and her descendants in his will. It was stipulated that this money was to be used for education only.

Hilda's mother often told Naomi stories of the old way of life, some handed down from the Zulu Wars of the late nineteenth century, but always fell short of explaining her affair with Peterson. She married some months after Peterson had died, and described an incident her husband had told her about. On his way back from a hunting trip he and four comrades came across three Boer infantry soldiers. They were wounded, but this did not deter the hunters and they murdered the white soldiers. Naomi's grandmother knew of the suffering and persecution of the black African at the hands of the Boer; it bred hatred and distrust but Beatrice could find no words to express her sadness at such an act. "Killing solves nothing and breeds hatred," she would tell her granddaughter.

Spontaneous as it was, Hilda tried to explain to Naomi at every opportunity that violence should not be met with violence; the old lady had seen plenty, the sadness etched on her face.

Naomi was fascinated with her grandmother. The one thing she really wanted to know had been swept under the carpet for years; it was something that the old lady never mentioned. It was difficult to break the family code of respect; she would need to wait until the time was right.

As a young girl, hiding in all the places little girls do provided Naomi with the opportunity to overhear discussions between family members that were not for the ears of the young. She did not understand all that was said but now, as she was becoming older, things were falling into place.

When Naomi looked in the mirror she saw a light brown face, and yet her family and friends in the village had a much darker tone to their skin. What was it that was in her bloodline, she asked herself?

When the elders talked late into the night they spoke about such things, and it was during one of these sessions that Naomi heard the old ladies talking and began to grasp the one tale that might provide the answer that she wanted.

By the time she reached fourteen Naomi was a magnificent specimen of a female – nearly six feet tall with a willowy torso and long legs that carried her like a gazelle. Her smile lit up the whole room.

One night she had been playing with friends in the open common area near her home, but the night was hot and she returned home early.

The rest of the family were out somewhere in the village when Naomi found herself sitting outside on the porch next to Beatrice. It was an ideal time to truly bond with her grandmother.

A QUIET TIME

They spoke softly; it was necessary because sound carried in the still night air. The old lady looked sad, and her eyes seemed to drift into another world. She chose her words carefully, describing her early life, the work she did, her family and the farm. She kept the discussion on the important issues of the time and did not dwell on detail. Her deep brown eyes stared at the light from the fire, and the flames reflected her every emotion: sadness, joy and trepidation.

Naomi needed to know the one thing that was on her mind – better to face it now, rather than never – but she might have to wait until Beatrice was ready.

"I was born at the turn of the century on a farm near the border of Zambia and Botswana," the old lady went on. "The owner of the farm was a Scotsman called Angus Peterson."

At this stage of the conversation Naomi started to suspect that he had been her mother's father, and this person that Beatrice was describing was her own biological grandfather, a white man. She could not wait to hear the whole story.

The old lady did not look up. "Peterson lived with his wife in the big house that his family had built a decade before. He told me later that he had watched me walking to the well for water, and he followed me everywhere, he became besotted. I am sure it was his age at the time to fancy a girl much younger than himself; it was the unbridled desire and lust that the old Scotsman had."

"How old was he at the time?" Naomi asked innocently.

"He and his wife were both in their late fifties." Beatrice paused. "Their relationship was now platonic, although still exceptionally friendly." She laughed. "I knew he always asked after me – where I was, when I would be back. He tried to be discreet; it did not always work but he found out what he needed to know.

"My mother and I had lived on the farm for three years, but during that time Peterson did not notice me. He could not understand why he hadn't known about me from the beginning – he later confided to me that those years had been wasted.

"When I started work at the farm his yard foreman made arrangements for me to move into a small house adjacent to the barn where my mother lived. I was to share with two other girls. My mother lived with her husband and another family in the converted barn.

"But one particular day Peterson was devious and sent two of the girls on a jaunt to the next farm to help with the harvest. This gave him the chance to visit me when I was alone. He told me later that he waited on the porch until his wife was in bed and all seemed quiet in the servants' quarters before he made his move.

"I was in turmoil when Peterson entered my room, undressed in the dark and climbed in beside me. I was numb with fright, too scared to cry out for my mother, who was so near but yet so far, and whilst he groped me I just gritted my teeth and lay still as he did what he wanted. His breath was thick with whisky fumes, and the pain was so intense; I did not understand his brutality at that time, as in later years he became gentle. I just winced through my tears, and at least it finished as quickly as it had started. Afterwards he got up, dressed without saying a word and left the hut.

"I lay very quiet and cried silently for many hours, feeling abused and alone. I was unable to call for help, too scared to shout for my mama – no one would believe me, so I just curled up.

"As I was falling into slumber, he returned, and I stiffened with horror. I closed my eyes, and then I smelt something and realised it was his whisky breath.

"'Do not say a word, for your sake and your mother's.' He paused. 'Do you understand?'

"Not opening my eyes, I said, 'Yes.'

"'Tell me you understand.' His tone was threatening.

"'Yes,' I replied again, 'I understand.'

"He had the hut sectioned off, with my small room nearest the main house, and this permitted him to visit me as much as he wanted. After a while he became more gentle, more humane, and even confided in me from time to time. I never fully accepted the situation but I did become tolerant as it brought some fruits of gain.

"However, he did not take precautions; it was not that he cared, but I knew it would cost him money in the long run both at the pregnancy stage and later when the child would need tending.

"I soon became pregnant and gave birth to a nine-pound baby girl who was to become your mother. Three years and one month after he had first visited me, Angus Peterson was killed, crushed by a tractor."

Beatrice laughed again, and the smile remained on her face when she said, "I smile with respect for Peterson, but must find immense amusement regarding the antics that occurred after his last will and testament was read by the local lawyer at the family gathering; the wailing and crying that ensued after we were bequeathed a portion of the inheritance. The whole of his family were disgusted, astounded that the old man would even consider us, the black worker, a stigma they could not contemplate; it would leave them in shame; but then I suppose we showed him the love and honesty that his family didn't.

"I put the money in a bank and split it to be shared by the next three generations, so a part of it can be used for your education, my dear."

"Thank you, Grandma, for your love, your generosity and sharing your stories. I love you."

The next day, armed with the information her grandmother had given her, Naomi approached her mother.

"Can I go to school here in Johannesburg?" she stammered, not knowing the family plans.

"No, my dear – your father and I are returning to Lundazi, and you will attend boarding school in Swaziland."

"Boarding school? Away from you and Papa?"

"Yes, my dear; you must get a good education, and this is private school, paid for by your inheritance that I understand your grandmother told you all about." Hilda smiled at her daughter. "It will provide a future for you. Now let's go inside before the lions eat us."

They both laughed. Naomi was now very excited about the future.

7

AN EDUCATION, 1966/67

Chaka wanted desperately to keep the family together, it was the Zulu way, but he secretly knew that a private school would be best for his daughter. Still, he maintained pretence just for appearances' sake, to maintain his pride within the family.

He did, however, discuss the situation with a local legal man, who advised him that education was the way forward for the black African. It was important to have a brain to compete in an ever-changing world, and this would be Naomi's opportunity.

Naomi herself was terrified but excited; she was to leave her beloved family, possibly for the next few years, staying with her uncle during midterm time and only returning home in the summer – a long time for a young girl to be away from her family.

She realised that it was a chance that many poor African children did not have, not even her brother or sisters, but she knew in her young mind that it was for the best.

She travelled alone by bus to Lusaka, and then took a two-hour flight to Maputo, where she would stay with her uncle for two nights before taking a bus for the last hundred miles to school. Maputo is predominantly a mining town, the most populated in Mozambique. Her uncle was a kind man and drove her in his rickety old car to the main bus station, where he dutifully shook her hand and bade her farewell as the bus started its journey to the town of Manzini, situated on the Swaziland border, close to her destination.

Naomi was truly exhausted when she arrived at her new school. She was relieved when the tedious task of registration was complete, and looked forward to some rest and recuperation.

She found the school very formal – scantily furnished and minimalistic, the wooden floors heavily polished, with wood continuing halfway up the walls. Above the wood the remaining walls and ceiling needed painting as the old paint was crumbling.

She shrugged and followed her tutor along the corridors, through double doors into a courtyard, then through a door into a long, prefabricated building.

"This is your dormitory, Naomi. Please find your bed; the fourth down the aisle to your right." The tutor smiled and beamed as she advised, "Mealtimes are on the noticeboard together with a timetable for your lessons. Have you any questions?"

"No, ma'am," Naomi answered politely.

Over the next few days Naomi found life strange. She felt that the whole school was avoiding her; perhaps it was her imagination but it seemed the other students were unsure of the tall and rangy girl who had just enrolled.

She kept her head high and her back straight; she was the daughter of Chaka, a descendant of the mighty Zulu chieftain, a fearless warrior. For the country girl from the backwoods of Lundazi, life was about to become more interesting.

The other students were a mixed bunch – different creeds, nationalities and colours – although all were privileged, born into families who could pay for their children to be educated. What better reason to send their offspring to a school in the bush and allow themselves the peace and tranquillity they wanted?

Naomi was fortunate; she was as tall as most adults, and

could utilise hand-me-downs from them. The quality of her clothes was questionable and did not reach the standard of the other pupils, but it was not the sort of thing that worried her. She was a happy girl and soon became popular with the other students, and at the school there was no prejudice: with black and white girls socialising with each other without a problem. She also learned from the playground a few African dialects such as Zulu, Bemba and Swahili, and in lessons developed her German and English, she was a quick learner.

The teachers all seemed relaxed; the teaching staff consisted of three female Zambian teachers, a male Ghanaian, a German and two South Africans, only the German and one of the Zambians were white.

The students were a mixture of colours and nationalities, and they all followed the rules of the school. After lights out many of them showed discontentment at being away from their families, especially the privileged ones who always complained about the conditions and the food. Naomi missed her mother and the slow pace of her village, but under the circumstances she was happy with her new situation.

One thing that caused her some discomfort was the Ghanaian teacher, a man called Nzema who always seemed to stare at her – in the recreation area, playing netball or just queuing at mealtimes, his stare was making life difficult. At first she shrugged it off, thinking it was her imagination, until the next time, when the situation started to unnerve her.

In Zambia and Swaziland there is no winter, only a dry and a wet season. The rains start in November, and the water runs off the hard land and quickly becomes a hazard to everything at a lower level. The school drains were ineffective due to lack of maintenance and flooded quickly; it was normal at this time of year and the pupils were trained to deal with the situation and form a chain gang to bail out the floodwater.

Due to the school being so close to the river and bush it was necessary to have a number of strict rules forbidding pupils from wandering outside the school boundaries. An abundant number of wild animals, both in the bush and in water, could take a child in a moment, and it was a daily drill for the teachers to lecture their students on this subject.

The river nearby flowed just outside the school grounds and when the water level was low tiger fish could be seen leaping; not a danger to the children in this case, but with crocodiles and hippopotamuses it was a different matter. Crocodiles lurked just under the water near the bank, always patient and waiting for the opportunity to strike quickly and drag their prey back into the water.

Hippopotamuses were a little different. Vegetarian, their power came from their size and temperament; they rampaged incessantly, and were normally most dangerous at night, hauling their huge bodies along the banks of the river, trampling anything that got in their way. An African social law related to this phenomenon: *One should never, ever get between the hippo and the river; it will run right over you.*

On one particular day after a brisk game of netball, Naomi was last in the shower and was enjoying the luxury of what she thought was privacy. Her smooth, beautiful body was lathered, her hair wet, and she was happy and the glint sparkled in her deep brown eyes. She rinsed her body and hair with clear water until all the soap was gone and finally opened her eyes, but was surprised to see two black African girls staring at her.

At first Naomi, feeling contented, ignored them, but, sensing an unnatural interest from them, decided to clarify the situation and strode naked towards them, as she did so swirling a towel around her body.

She spoke in English rather than the Bemba language. With her customary direct attitude, she looked down at the girls. "What are you two staring at?" she asked, towering above them.

The girls were nervous and stammered, each hoping that the other would be the leader.

"Well?" Naomi looked imposing.

The girls remained quiet, although transfixed.

Naomi tried to cover herself with the small towel. "What is the matter with the two of you? Do I have to slap a response out of you?" She was amazed at her own aggressiveness.

The smaller of the two girls answered timidly, "My name is Rose, and we apologise for embarrassing you. So sorry." She waited for a moment, and without looking at Naomi stammered, "Our bodies appear different than yours."

"What do you mean, different?" hissed Naomi.

"You are beautiful, but may not find a man to marry later," Rose stammered.

"Not find a man, what is that all about?" Naomi did not understand.

"The elders in our tribe say women must make themselves attractive to men by pulling down here." And she demonstrated a pulling movement in her loins.

Naomi realised what they were saying, and laughed for the first time since the conversation began. "Then you must listen to your elders because they are wise, but as for me, I am happy. I do not want a husband, especially if he dictates how I look, but let us be friends." She extended her hand in friendship and gave the two smaller girls a good hug. Both sighed with relief as they looked up at their new friend.

"Let's get dressed and go for something to eat." Naomi continued to smile at the smaller girls. She thought that school was becoming more interesting by the day.

Quietly and compassionately, Naomi mothered the two girls from then on, protecting them, talking to them in the evening before lights out. The school was large, with about three hundred pupils, of whom thirty-five were in Naomi's class. Her studies progressed and she qualified for taking the matriculation examination. Her prowess in sport, mainly because of her size, surpassed anything the school had seen before. She was selected for sporting honours and played for the Zambian schools' national netball team. Her life was at an exciting threshold.

But there was a dark shadow lurking over her, in the form of the Ghanaian teacher who seemed to be stalking her constantly; during her outdoor sports sessions and at her study breaks in the courtyard. He was becoming a worry.

8

A REUNION AT MI6, 1ST MAY 1981

All the great rivers around the world can tell a story. They flow and ebb and are the core of the city they dominate. The River Thames in London is no different.

The horror and tragedy that spur notoriety over hundreds of years become bizarrely attractive to city tourists. These grim reminders of bad deeds that happened long ago were not in the visitors' minds on this beautiful spring day in 1981. The river was alive with colour, pleasure boats purred up and down between Greenwich and their city moorings, and hundreds of tourists walked along the Embankment, enjoying the sun and festivities. City workers hurried about their business as though there wasn't a moment to lose, dodging tourists and carrying loaded briefcases, sweltering under the hot May Day sun and keeping cool the best way that they could.

George Webster, an MI6 agent, had over the past few years built up an established information network, mostly from the ordinary public. Although it was an invaluable source, it was often sensationalised and unreliable. Today he left his flat in the South London suburb of Balham dressed in a light suit. He was without any topcoat, and felt he was dressed adequately for the mild weather.

After departing the Tube at Waterloo, he walked along Westminster Bridge Road and slowed down to collect his thoughts, organising his mind for the day ahead. By the time he reached the office steps he was perspiring; his thoughts had cost him dearly, for he was now behind on his personalised schedule.

In precisely fifteen minutes he was to attend a meeting concerning security arrangements for the opening ceremony at Sullom Voe, the oil terminal in Shetland. HM The Queen was to officiate but other dignitaries would accompany her including her husband the Duke of Edinburgh, and King Olav of Norway. This meeting had been called due to information George had received from a worker at the site, and the event had subsequently been put on red alert.

The date for the opening ceremony was the 9th May 1981, and to make matters a little more complicated than just dealing with one perpetrator, George had also received unsubstantiated evidence that the KGB had taken an interest in activities at the oil terminal.

Leonid Brezhnev had succeeded Nikita Khrushchev as leader of the Soviet Union in 1964. He and his communist regime continued to survive, but the Russian public were being influenced by Western capitalism, and unrest within the ranks was spreading through the whole of the Soviet Union.

To make matters worse, Lech Wałęsa headed the Solidarity movement in Poland, a powerful non-governmental trade union that started in 1980 in the shipyards of the country. It was the first independent labour movement in the Soviet Bloc and claimed nearly ten million members. The Pope supported Wałęsa, and Solidarity were later to have a major impact in the fall of communism in the Soviet Bloc.

His Eminence Pope John Paul II was a popular figure throughout most of the civilised countries, gaining respect and admiration worldwide. His stance against the Soviets was intense and they were becoming impatient with him. He wanted religious freedom for all countries within the Soviet Union, and especially for his native Poland.

9

DOUBLE TROUBLE, MAY 1981

Michael O'Byrne was suspected of being a double agent working for both the KGB and the Irish Republican Army. He was subsequently arrested on his way to Sullom Voe in 1979, but later released from police custody in December 1980 due to lack of evidence. O'Byrne started his campaign by securing work with the terminal operator (client), and soon after being accepted made plans to visit the site.

Unfortunately, whilst he was waiting for a flight from Glasgow to Shetland, Glasgow Police and the Security Services intercepted him. As further information was received it became apparent that O'Byrne was indeed involved with both the IRA and the KGB.

In gathering further information, it transpired that a further IRA cell was suspected to be active in the Shetlands, involving two suspects. One remained unknown; the other had been confirmed as Barney Coughlin, a construction worker on the site. In July 1980 Coughlin absconded from Shetland before any serious damage was done, but the full relevance of both O'Byrne and Coughlin was being considered.

Webster had prepared his agenda. O'Byrne had been in custody but released due to lack of evidence, and his movements were now carefully monitored. Coughlin, on the other hand, needed to be located and arrested as soon as possible, before the IRA got to him.

The highest priority at the opening ceremony was to ensure that HM The Queen and her entourage were safe at all times.

The director general walked past George as he departed the lift. "Everything in order, Webster, eh?" He paused for a second, and before George could answer continued, "Call me when all personnel are here, and let's get this thing started."

"I will check now and let you know, sir."

"Good man." And the director general strode onwards to his office and shut the door.

The meeting was well attended, with a representative from each major unit, when George entered he made a mental note of all personnel in attendance and assured himself that all invited were present.

Those represented covered MI5, Shetland Constabulary, Ulster Constabulary, Glasgow Constabulary, and Martin Ellis from Special Forces. Ellis was best known for his cunning and his unscrupulous methods in dealing with the most difficult investigations.

All were seated when the director general entered the room and closed the door behind him. He did not sit, but stood erect, not even reviewing his notes. "I will not beat about the bush. If anything goes wrong with this event in the Shetlands, heads will roll. Today you will not advise me on what needs to be done; but give me the answer; it has been done. He quickly scrutinised his notes. "Give me all the information on O'Byrne and Coughlin and advise me if one or both are still active. I am to understand that at least one other terror suspect is in operation in the Shetlands; are these direct replacements for O'Byrne and Coughlin?"

"Coughlin has not yet been located and we understand he has a replacement now in operation, yet unknown." Ellis informed the meeting.

He went on. "O'Byrne departed the country for the Soviet Bloc but we have no information on his whereabouts to date."

The director general looked around the room. He made eye contact with each of the attendees, and it wasn't as much staring as glaring. "Do not speculate unnecessarily; there may be many suspects but do not waste time on scraps of information that lead to nowhere. We must have enough information to nail the culprits. If there is nothing else, I will bid you good day and remind you that the next meeting is in two weeks' time, on the 14th May to be precise."

THAT EVENING...

It was a chic restaurant close to King's Cross Station, and George Webster and Sean O'Leary, the chief inspector of the Ulster Constabulary, were ushered to a table in a quiet part of the restaurant.

"Is this dinner on your expenses or mine?" The chief inspector was being facetious.

"I will pay for the meal if you get the drinks, Sean." George, pretending to read the menu, was waiting for a satisfactory reply.

"All depends what we drink, I guess," joked the inspector.

"It's not what we drink, as my expenses will not cover alcohol," said George.

"Make the wine reasonable and I am in." And they shook hands and laughed.

George became serious. "Our man Coughlin, have you checked him out?" he queried.

"Absolutely, my friend; he was brought up a good Catholic altar boy, took up boxing and won more fights than he lost; he boxed out of Warrenpoint Amateur Boxing Club. After school he was taken on as an apprentice at a garage and reports are that he was an excellent mechanic. No regular girlfriends, liked a beer but nothing big, and he was the last of his mates to leave for greener fields – well, joint last, as he left with one of them, a lad called Declan."

"Can we pick him up? It's bloody important that he does not pull the trigger." Sean was firm.

George interrupted. "Why do we not know of this situation, Sean? Is this Secret Squirrel or something?"

"George, we have just found this out; it will be in our report to you guys in about a week."

"And this Declan, have you checked him out on site?"

"Yes we have, and he is clean, apparently not even socialised with his friend Coughlin." Sean sounded confident.

"I must act now and get a tag on him, see what he is up to." George sat back in thought.

"Remember what your boss stated. Do not waste time on unproven information; it'll lead to the same embarrassment as what happened to O'Byrne."

"Agreed: holding a man without evidence has a limit."

"Well, what are we drinking? I am hungry and thirsty." Sean laughed.

George broke from deep thought. "It's the halibut and a red; I'm for the Italian Barolo '66."

They both were deep in thought.

"By the way, George, how do we know that Coughlin is the man we want? I understand that there was an Irishman called Barney who suddenly absconded from the site – or are they one and the same?"

The waiter brought the Barolo, showed Sean the label and poured a taster drop into his glass.

"That fine."

The waiter poured a little more into George's glass, and they clinked before each tippled.

"They are the same person; it was a report that I received from an informant."

"What did the report suggest?"

"Overheard a conversation and put a name to a face."

"That's not a strong case," said Sean.

"I know that, but we have a number of other pointers – need to follow them up," advised Webster.

The halibut was served and they both fell silent as they sampled the fish.

"What has been done about finding him?" said Webster.

"We have scoured the Shetlands, and are now doing the same in mainland Scotland, but London is for someone else to handle."

"Who is covering that?"

"Your man Martin Ellis, and working with you," Sean advised.

"That's interesting; well, he hasn't contacted me yet." George was thoughtful. "By the way, I will skip dessert and have a coffee with a brandy instead." He laughed.

It was late when they parted at the door of the restaurant.

"Sean, please advise me of any titbits when you hear them and I will do the same, OK?"

"Absolutely, I'll do that."

They shook hands and went their separate ways.

10

NEVER SAY GOODBYE, SPRING 1981

The British winter of 1981 was typical: cold, damp, a sprinkle of snow, but nothing over the top.

Barney was about to make his move. It wasn't because he was unhappy or threatened, but he couldn't live the life of a fugitive in hiding. This is what it felt like to him, cooped up in Sarah's house during the day and scurrying out wrapped up like a mummy at night.

His association with her remained very good, but it seemed to Barney that their association was more like a 'friend with benefits' rather then a serious love affair. They slept together only sparingly, Barney returning to his bed after the few times when they had the need.

Sarah was attentive and loving, suspecting that some day Barney would go, so she made the most of it while it lasted, and when it did it was free and uninhibited.

Barney was aware of her feelings, and it was no easy task for him to plan a departure in June. The remaining few weeks would give him ample time to fine-tune his movements.

His thoughts occupied him most of the day as he continually reviewed his plans. It had taken him a long time and his research provided him with the direction he would take; he had decided to head for Africa. For what reasons, he wasn't sure, but he felt that it was easier to lose oneself there than on any other continent, and of course for the majority of Africa's countries, the language spoken was English.

He plotted the places of uncertainty and the risk they carried; these included the ports of Dover into France and Spain into Morocco; each of the borders here might disclose him as a fugitive. The towns of Tarifa and Algeciras had ferry schedules that sailed to Tangier, and were close to the busy British colony of Gibraltar. The non-ferry-terminal towns were a risk to Barney for different reasons; Gibraltar patrolled by British police and the town of La Linear for its lawlessness. He may need to consider the best option for lying low if the situation arose.

Barney's opinion was that travel in Africa may be more straightforward, and that the border guards would be less meticulous and easier to bribe than those in Europe and the Far East. He had ascertained that his problem would be his own personal safety – most of the countries would be poor and life there cheap; if people knew he carried money it would be especially dangerous. He would need to carry less than he'd originally planned and use the local banks whenever necessary.

The timing of his journey should match the good weather of the northern hemisphere at this time, and he could not wait to get started. He chose the 1st June, and on a damp and cold day left Sarah's house when she was out meeting friends. He left her a brief note that was tender and personal. It read:

Living here with you was nice. You are my closest friend in the world and I will never forget you. When I write, please destroy the evidence, and I hope we can meet again sometime in the future.
Barney

Five weeks later, Barney stepped from the train in Casablanca and headed for the Rendi Hotel; it was not the best place to stay in town but it shouldn't attract attention, and the staff were not expected to ask too many questions.

NEW NAME, NEW PERSON?

As Charles stood in line waiting to check in to the hotel, he glanced at the passport in his hand. Subconsciously he had opened it ready to be inspected, and his thumb marked the page with his photograph. It seemed strange that his name was now Charles Siddons, no longer Barney Coughlin. This he would need to get used to!

He left the hotel the next morning, passing through airport security without a hitch, then boarded a plane heading for Lubumbashi, a town situated deep in Africa in the southern part of the Democratic Republic of the Congo. During his research whilst planning his journey he had ascertained that the short journey from Lubumbashi to Konkola in Zambia should not be a problem, and he thought this could be done by hired car or taxi.

However, it was his opinion that crossing the border into Zambia from the French-speaking Democratic Republic of the Congo may be a problem, and as a precaution he made sure that he was carrying enough cash to overcome resistance by way of a 'dash' or 'bung'. Charles intended to keep his ears and eyes wide open and look for the opportunities if and when they came. He thought that if problems did arise, there was more chance that they would come from the DRC side due to the language barrier.

He passed at border control at Lubumbashi without a hitch; none of the officers on duty seemed to care and waved him through. But his mood changed when he saw the state of the taxis waiting to be hired; they all looked ready for the scrapheap and he was sure they would not make the Zambian border, and he did not much feel like camping out in the African bush. All, of them were decrepit, old and rusty vehicles; he had inspected each one and they all looked totally unsafe and not fit to be on the road.

He needed to get more information from the car rental information kiosk and waited for the clerk to return. It was over half an hour before she arrived.

"Can you advise me on the best way to travel over the border to Konkola?" He waited for an answer, wondering whether she would offer him the advice he wanted.

The pretty black lady pulled out of her desk drawer a bunch of leaflets and papers, and explained to Charles the procedure and cost. "It would be better if you hired a taxi; the cost of car rental is expensive, especially if you intend to drive over the border. The rental company will almost certainly require a bond."

"Can I hire a taxi from here?

"You can, but it will be better if you hire one from outside the departure lounge. You will also need a visa from the government, that is, to enter Zambia."

"How long will that take?" Charles asked

"Three days normally, but if we send our courier it will take only a day," the lady advised.

"How much?" Charles asked.

"Fifty dollars, American."

"Can you get it for me today and I will pay you double?" Charles laughed.

"We can try, if you want." The lady tabled the papers, wrote a note on plain paper and called a young youth from the back of the office, gave him instructions and passed him the note with the cash.

The Democratic Republic of the Congo (DRC) was granted independence from Belgium in 1960. It took only four years for their first despot to become president, when Mobutu Sese Seko won a supposedly rigged election, and it took another thirty-two years for another despot, Laurent-Désiré Kabila, to oust him from power.

During his reign Mobutu was accused of many unlawful acts including human rights abuses, money laundering, and corruption on a huge scale: he was rumoured to have extracted four billion dollars from the economy and transferred it to his personal Swiss bank account. It was the equivalent close to the Zambian national debt at the time. Ordinary people suffered immense hardship, food was scarce and work hard to come by, and the roads and security were controlled by a corrupt police force, their wages paid for by the fines they imposed on the public.

When Charles tried to negotiate his taxi fare from Lubumbashi Airport, there were fifty drivers all offering different rates. He would get a discount if he paid in American dollars.

During his flight he had studied the map of the Zambian towns close to the border. The best one to stay in would be either Chililabombwe or Konkola; he would make that decision when he arrived.

Finally, he agreed a rate of one hundred dollars paid in advance. He wondered if he would reach Konkola alive, as this must be the most decrepit car on the planet; nevertheless, he collected his bag and they were off.

The journey seemed long and arduous and after three hours of hard, scary driving they arrived at the border. But his luck left him when, after queuing for an hour, he was held by border control, who claimed that Charles had a visa problem. It was explained in detail why he was in breach of the regulations, pointing out the parts of his visa that did not match those on his passport.

"What do you mean, 'do not tie up'?"

The officials remained dogmatic. The visa for entry to the DRC was not the correct one, and it was obvious they wanted to be convinced it was right before they even addressed his Zambian documents.

He approached the officer, who waved him to the side, away from the rest of the passengers disembarking.

"So what do you want from me to pass into Zambia?" asked Charles.

"You must go back to Lubumbashi and re-clarify your details."

"You must be joking. Can I pay for you to verify my visa here and now?" he pleaded.

The officer stood between Charles and the next passenger, who was becoming agitated. "I can, but it will take time and is a costly business."

"How much is 'costly', in dollars?"

"It will be four hundred dollars, but can only be done after all passengers have passed through."

A passenger who was waiting some way down the line moved up and stood within talking distance of the officer and Charles. He was over six feet tall, his sleeveless vest emphasised his muscular physique, and his face was thin and hard. He hadn't shaved for a few days. "What is the trouble? Can I be of assistance?"

The officer, on seeing the man, suddenly stiffened. His attitude changed, and he suddenly began to show signs of nervousness. "His passport is not in order. It will need to be verified and amended, but this cannot be done until tomorrow, as the chief officer is not available until then."

Charles interrupted. "They want four hundred dollars to 'revise' the visa."

"Enough." The tall man glared at the officer. "My name is George Mwanza, you know that. Let this man through; I will talk with Benson in the morning."

"But—" the officer protested.

"No. As I said, tomorrow."

The two of them walked through from the airside and stopped to chat on the Zambian side of the border.

George Mwanza looked at the grateful Charles. "Look, boss," he said. "You owe me, but I will just take 250 dollars now and pay you back in a month."

"You want me to lend you 250 dollars?" Charles wanted confirmation of what he was hearing.

"Yes. But as I said, I will pay it back in a month; I will have a deal through by then."

Charles asked George to wait whilst he went to the money services, and within five minutes returned and gave George the 250 American dollars. "You do not owe me anything, George; that was a good deal, and I am grateful."

The man looked down at Charles. His face was set, with not a smile or any other sign of feeling. "As I said, it is a loan. Where will you stay in Zambia?"

"I don't know, probably Ndola."

"I know your name and will find you, but now I must be off." Then George quickly turned his attention to two very colourful females who were waiting for him.

11

NDOLA: A PLACE TO REMEMBER, SUMMER 1981

The backpack that Charles had hauled all the way from London weighed a ton and he wondered why it seemed heavier now than when he had left, which seemed a hundred years ago.

He headed for the small guest house he had pre-booked, checked in, and fell onto the bed without undressing. Tomorrow would be another day, he thought; first he would sleep, and then make plans for his travel tomorrow. He was hoping to visit Ndola and see if the town was suitable to set up his temporary home.

It now seemed a million years ago that he had researched and selected these places to stay en route. He wondered what had endeared them to him when he learned of them at the travel agent, but he was thankful they had.

The Zambian climate is renowned as one of the best in the world; never a winter, only a wet and a dry season, a good quality of air. As he lay on the bed he tried to remember the geographic statistics of the country. They had a low of one thousand feet and a high of seven thousand feet above sea level, and he remembered that Ndola was at three thousand feet and had good air quality.

On balance it was very acceptable, even if the smelting plants belonging to the Copperbelt mines were taken into account, and with all these numbers bouncing around his head he fell asleep, only to wake with a start an hour before dawn, but then settled back and listened to the sounds outside.

It was unnerving for him to hear these strange noises, different than any he had heard before; it was only the dogs barking that reminded him of home. He assumed the incessant chirping was perhaps crickets; the short, high-pitched calls he suspected were monkeys, but the action was not all outside; it was also the consistent buzzing of mosquitoes outside his protective nets. He wondered what would happen if all those mosquitoes suddenly got inside the net and sucked his blood at the same time. He wondered if the noises he could hear were worse than those things he could not hear; those silent killers one comes across in a nightmare.

As he lay there resting, he realised for the first time since going to bed that all the other guests in the house were silent. Yet at three o'clock it had seemed as if the hotel was the centre of a railway station, with continuous noise from people's footsteps, incessant talking, a steady hum of voices from dusk to nearly dawn, and it was during this time that he'd felt alone, and scared.

Life was cheap in Africa; gangs would kill, rob and rape at any time; certainly a wooden door was not going to stop any predators. They could burst into his room in a moment and cut him in half with a panga; it did not bear thinking about.

He was glad to wake in the morning in one piece, the sun streaming through the window. The fear had gone.

CHARLES GOES WALKABOUT

A few days after arriving at Ndola, Charles wanted to get out and about to see what the place was like, even make a few friends. Those people he had met already all seemed to be friendly and hospitable; probably, he thought, they were of the same ilk as George Mwanza. He too was friendly, so much so that he had been able to fleece Charles out of a few hundred dollars.

The first thing he needed to do was to check out the municipality where he now lived – the shops, roads, administration buildings, bus station and airport. It was necessary to know where the primary buildings were situated, including the police station, the best pubs, the town hall and the long-haul bus station. He had been told by the boys in the bar to avoid travelling in the white transit vans used as taxis; they said if he did it may be the last time he travelled anywhere. The township people would see to that.

Nevertheless, he liked the area and if he did settle in Ndola he hoped he could do business in the social climate, perhaps find a house and negotiate the terms without providing his personal details.

He shaved and showered, and thought it would be nice to dress smartly, but looking at his pile of crumpled clothes in his backpack he thought there wasn't much chance of that. He would take them to the launderette tomorrow, but for now he would test out the mood of the people.

As he approached the Savoy Hotel, it was obvious by the flaking paint hanging from the walls that it had seen better days. The traffic passing on the road was now much busier than earlier in the day; it seemed that the working class were on their way home, and the drinkers on their way to the hotel.

Once he had reached the inn and entered the bar area, he found himself amongst a noisy bunch of local guys enjoying a drink. It was a national holiday and the bar was full of mineworkers, with hardly enough space left for a lone drinker, and the noise in the room was so loud it was difficult for the barman to hear Charles's order.

Although the mood was boisterous, it was affable; the people seemed a peaceful lot and, seeing a new white face enter their space, they soon befriended him.

"Where do you come from, man?" shouted a huge black worker. He was only three feet away from Charles but anyone who heard him would have thought he was communicating with someone fifty yards away. After every gulp of beer, he slammed the bottle on a nearby table and the beer frothed over and dripped onto the floor.

"From Ireland," answered Charles, but he felt guilty and did not offer any more than this.

"From where? I thought an island was a place in the middle of the ocean," queried the big man.

Charles changed the subject and hoped that the man would forget where his original track had been going. "Would you like another beer, friend?"

"Yes, man, that would be great; I will ask the barman to bring them over. One for me and three others for my friends here; let me introduce them."

He turned to three characters similar in looks to himself; they were all in conversation but when the words 'another drink' were uttered they stopped talking (or shouting) and paid attention to the big man.

"I am Issac." He looked down to at the others. "This is Boniface, and John, and the good-looking one is Lotte."

"Hi, guys, hope you're well and enjoy the drink; it is a pleasure to meet you all."

They all nodded in unison and their smiles seemed to reflect their appreciation for the beers.

"Where are you living?" asked Issac, swaying on his feet as he waited for an answer.

"At the guest house on the Kitwe road," said Charles, "but I am looking for something more permanent." He was careful to

65

hold back any information that would lead the others to think about his originality.

"Just a minute, boss, I may have something for you." Issac moved towards the bar and shouted to the barman, who was pouring a beer into a glass. "Jacob, are you still looking to rent your house?"

"Yes, man, but keep your voice down; I do not want the whole world to hear." He winked, and it suggested something about the proposed transaction was not normal.

Issac continued the conversation as the barman closed the till and moved towards Charles. "This white guy needs a place to stay; he is writing a book and it may take a year or so. You know, man, it's good business, and you know one good deed needs a return."

"OK, OK, but let me do a deal first and keep your mouth shut."

"OK, then speak with him." Issac shouted to Charles and waved him over. "Charles, please meet Jacob; he has something to offer you."

At midnight Charles staggered from the hotel bar. His mind was scrambled, his legs were like jelly and he held the building wall; he was sure without support he might well fall on his face.

He collected his thoughts. Where was his bloody guesthouse?

"How will you get back to your boarding house?" Issac slurred from the hotel door.

"Can I get a taxi?" asked Charles.

"Not if you value your life."

"What, then?"

"Stay with me," the local man slurred, then added, "just for the night, and you better leave when I go to work at five o'clock, otherwise the neighbours will talk about a white man alone in the house with my wife."

Barney felt content in Ndola; he had made friends on his first night out and, although he'd got plastered doing it, in the morning he still remembered to pay the deposit and one month's rent to his landlord. His head was throbbing!

One thing was missing from his rejuvenated life: sport. His friends from the bar were no help; they only had an association with football and boxing. His enquiries led people to advise him to approach the expat community, and he did; the local vicar informed him there were three decent expat clubs that sponsored polo, tennis and golf.

The following day he was obtaining references to join the golf club.

12

FINDING A NEEDLE IN A HAYSTACK, 1ST MAY 1981

The tall, balding man was gazing out of his Manhattan hotel window. His stomach was hanging over his belt and his silhouetted outline looked even more rotund than he actually was. His face was grey and he did not look happy – he was about to discuss a particularly embarrassing situation with the two colleagues sitting behind him.

McGirk was the commander of the South Armagh division of the IRA, and it was his brigade who, in August 1979, had carried out two horrendous attacks simultaneously.

Today McGirk was nervous; in two weeks' time members of his brigade would attempt the IRA's most outrageous attack on the British Queen and on the same day an organisation called the Grey Wolves were planning to assassinate John Paul II, and, if both attacks were to be successful, the consequences of the bombings would shock the world.

The operation was monumental; the two-pronged attack was brokered by the IRA and sponsored by the KGB. It would be the most audacious in the history of the IRA, and the Soviet Secret Service hoped it would unstable Europe and change the minds of the Russian people and take them away from their own problems of discontentment. All necessary arrangements had been made and it was only days until the attack. All those concerned were on edge, and none more so than McGirk.

It was a setback that one of the main agents had absconded six months before the date. The IRA had responded quickly and replaced him with one of their best men; there was no change to the 9th May 1981, and everything was in hand.

McGirk addressed the meeting, "Brothers, I need to know whether this Coughlin still lives. Is he active? And can he bring harm to the brigade?"

O'Donnell was the first to answer. "We have lost him, only temporarily, but we're almost sure that he is currently in hiding in the London area. We have plenty of workers in the city who have their noses to the floor; they will surely pick up a lead soon."

McGirk drew a deep breath. "It doesn't matter; it would appear that so far he has kept his mouth shut, nothing seems to have transpired relating to him, so I guess he is inactive."

McInerney broke the silence. "If he has spoken with the police we will not know until the day."

"That is too fucking late, and Declan and Billy will be doing twenty years by then."

"What do we do, call the thing off?" queried O'Donnell.

There was quiet. After a long pause, McGirk turned away from the window and sat down heavily on an armchair. "We cannot; it is a dual operation with the Soviets and now it's too late – we would not only lose face but may acquire other enemies that we certainly do not want at the present moment."

McGirk held a hand up to his forehead, in deep thought. The other two said nothing and waited. Then he perked up and gestured to O'Donnell. "You get back to Belfast and see what you can do regarding a backup, just in case the plan goes tits up. Don't forget that we are on the edge, there's not much

69

time." He was perspiring as he turned to McInerney. "And you, put the word around regarding our friend Coughlin; someone knows where this guy is. I need to stay here, both for an alibi and for army business. Keep the pressure on your duties; we certainly need to be smart, as the feds are hitting us hard." McGirk continued to stare at McInerney. "Find this man quickly."

"And if we find him?" he answered.

"Needs to be a summary. But no evidence, do you understand?"

"OK, we will do what is necessary," McInerney confirmed.

"And by the way, if it turns out that this man Coughlin keeps his mouth shut we may take the heat off him. Keep him in mind, you understand, but do not commit people to look for him when it is not necessary." McGirk seemed flustered.

"Then we need to find him now to reduce future risks."

"That's right. Phone me if you have a problem."

O'Donnell and McInerney opened the door carefully to ensure that the coast was clear, then silently slipped out.

McGirk waited, and when the door was closed he picked up the telephone and dialled a number. "Billy, is that you?"

McGirk was calling Billy Keogh who was one of the best bomb makers in the IRA. He was the replacement for Barney Coughlin at Sullom Voe.

"To be sure it's me." Billy was being mischievous.

"How are the preparations going?"

"Fine."

"How fine?"

"Well, it's difficult to get close at the moment due to security but we are getting there."

"What are the difficulties?"

"Access and delivery."

"Access?"

"The stage is too open, difficulty in selecting a spot, but we are working on it; may have to go further away with a bigger blast."

"OK, and delivery?"

"Yes, we are waiting to collect at the post depot, but cannot keep asking the postman, he may get wind, so find out when it will come."

"OK, I will. How many are you expecting?"

"Two big ones."

"OK, I will chase up. Keep at it."

"By the way, any sign of Coughlin?"

"In a word, no." McGirk felt exposed.

"OK, must go." Billy sounded impatient.

"See you." McGirk put the phone down gently.

13

FORBIDDEN LIAISON, 1967/68

Kwasi Nzema was forty years of age. He had originally graduated from Accra University with a degree in communications (English), and since then had travelled around, working his way through various colleges and universities in Africa.

This tall and bespectacled man had a reputation as a womaniser, but anyone who met him would have thought he was far from the Casanova type. Generally well liked in college circles, his energy and enthusiasm earned him a good reputation.

This reputation did not reflect his dark side, his fascination with a female pupil; it was totally outside the bounds of his most wayward thought; it did not bear the slightest resemblance to the basic rules between a teacher at a junior school and pupil. A girl under the age of consent, a forbidden relationship – it was a problem on the greatest scale; one that could finish his career or under the rules of the village even his life. This tall, beautiful student was always in his mind; dangerous to him and totally illegal. This did not deter him; he was heading for disaster.

Just two months before the end of term Kwasi made his first move by approaching the wife of one of his teaching colleagues. He had previously been associated with this woman; their sordid affair lasted but a few months and they now only shared 'things' in common. He discussed the situation with her, his plans for hosting a small party at her house on the day after school finished for the holiday. Her husband agreed with his wife and they rented the house to Kwasi for two nights; she stipulated that any comeback from those two days would be his responsibility.

Naomi would be invited to the party on the pretext that it was a going-away celebration following her success at Standard 8, leading up to matriculation at Standard 10.

For Kwasi the time leading up to the school holidays passed slowly, but when the last day of term finally arrived he paid the rent and waited to prepare the house for his 'party'. He then rearranged the furniture, closed all the curtains and blinds to make it as secluded as possible, then carefully arranged drinks and snacks on the long sideboard.

Expecting Naomi at any moment, he dashed upstairs, showered and put on a casual open-necked shirt. It hung over his trousers in a youthful fashion, and he was ready to meet his next conquest.

Sitting down on the long sofa, it wasn't long before he heard movement outside, and at about seven o'clock she passed the window, followed a few seconds later by a restrained knock at the door. He waited a few moments.

"Hello, Naomi, I was not sure whether I would recognise you in your going-away clothes. You look beautiful, and welcome." Kwasi spoke with the assurance of an older man. "I am afraid we are the only two people left for the party; all the others have not been able to come for one reason or another, and it would be a shame to waste the food and drink." Kwasi reeled off the excuses for the other four guests, and at the same time ushered Naomi into the lounge.

Although a respected teacher within the school Naomi did not trust him based on his previous behaviour. She also knew that if he became aggressive and she screamed for help it was her opinion that people would only believe his version of the story.

He did not take long to show her the house, and the conversation wilted when they reached the bedroom. He shut the door quietly and took off his shirt.

She moved towards the door, she was both scared but still worried if she shouted and then was accused of being rude to the teacher.

"Come, child." He touched her arm gently and stroked her hair. She felt uncomfortable and asked Kwasi to let her go to the bathroom; he held her, and told her she could go in a while.

Slowly but forcefully he undressed her, and she froze in terror. His tone and actions became agitated and he pushed her onto the bed. The whole process of his seduction seemed to last an eternity and the act left her scared and disgusted.

Later in the evening he fell asleep, and she wasted no time in collecting her clothes and slipping out of the house. Dishevelled and scared, she did not stop until she reached the bus stop, where she sat down and sobbed for hours, not even noticing that it was now early morning.

Just as the morning was breaking and light could be seen over the distant sky, some miners, worse for drink from the night before, passed her. In a kind but slurred tone of voice, they asked if everything was OK. She told them that she was all right, but had missed the bus the night before and was waiting for the first of the day. They showed no emotion, nodded and moved on towards their destination.

The time was passing slowly it was a long night, and so tired she fell asleep and woke up periodically, and was grateful she was awake when the bus arrived; it was 6.30 in the morning. In a daze she paid her fare, fell into a double seat and immediately fell into a deep slumber. She remained in this state for many hours, but then as if by magic she stood up. Her destination approached and her demeanour changed; she came alive. It was

74

another day, this time for love, kisses and hugs from everyone who would welcome her home, especially her mother. But before she could experience this, there would be a flight to Lusaka and then another bus. She thought that when she arrived at the village all this travelling would be worth it.

14

A FRIEND SO NEAR IS NOT ALWAYS SO DEAR, MAY 1980

The old Zambia Airways Boeing 707 bumped down at Lusaka Airport, and Martin Valeron stepped out from the plane and into the bright African sunlight. The airport was chaotic and he finally pushed his way through the vibrant crowd into the reception area and sought out his next flight to Kitwe.

He waited for an hour before boarding, and the flight was scheduled to take an hour, so it was a respite when he fell asleep for the duration.

At Kitwe Airport he was glad to see his old friend from Sullom Voe, a funny and fun-loving man by the name of Geoff de Kok. He wore his normal cheeky grin his innocent face giving nothing away to his true character and the dangerous practical jokes that he could play.

The ex-public schoolboy had lost none of his boyish ways, but Martin was glad to hear his rich and mature British accent wafting across the airport.

As a former colleague Geoff had arrived in Kitwe six weeks earlier. This was to cover for Martin, who had been retained at Sullom Voe for a suitable handover period from the job he was leaving.

"Hope that you had a good journey, old boy, plenty of rest, because you will be busy during the next couple of years."

It was May 1980 and the rains had yet to come; the terrain on the way from the airport was dry and the dust was churned up by the truck, not helped by de Kok's erratic driving.

"I am tired, the flight was bloody hard; all I want to do is rest," explained Martin.

"You do not need too much sleep, that's for old people, and you will only end up with jet lag. I will settle you in the guest house – it's an old VD clinic converted for expatriate workers, quite comfortable – and then this evening I will introduce you to my friends at the yacht club." Geoff was buoyant, and his attitude had not changed.

"Yacht club? What is this, a bloody holiday camp?" stammered Martin.

"Your job is going to be hard. You know – ordering and delivery of equipment for the cobalt plant is difficult in this part of the world, client not paying his bills, delays incorrect delivery of plant, otherwise this place is wonderful."

"How do you mean, wonderful?" asked Martin.

"Weather is the best in the world, every sports club in the town is tailored to suit one's interest, although food is scarce, there is nothing in the supermarket." Geoff shrugged and went on. "That's why I want to show you the yacht club. I have reserved a single scull for you later; have you done any sailing before?"

"No, I haven't; we didn't have the facilities at my school, unlike your posh set-up." Martin was sarcastic.

They pulled up at a large white house and Geoff jumped out, quickly offloading Martin's suitcase, whilst Martin quickly exited the vehicle. Then Geoff jumped straight back in and departed in a hail of dust, shouting, "Pick you up at five."

REST AND RECUPERATION

The yacht club looked serene as Martin manoeuvred the old vehicle along the unmade road, through two huge gates and into the evening sun.

"Pull to the left, Martin, and we will leave this old thing here whilst I take you to the skiff." Geoff was his old youthful, exuberant self. "Lovely building, don't you think, old boy? Colonial style, that's for sure! The type constructed by expats back some hundred or so years ago, and in those days everything was built to Commonwealth standards; fit for a king, you know what I mean? Come, I'll show you inside."

The building had a grand entrance with two large double doors. Inside the stairs were large and grand and wound up to the first floor. At the foot of the stairs, to the right, a double door led to an open bar with a panoramic view of the lake outside. To the left of the stairs, opposite the bar, a corridor wound through to the rear of the clubhouse. Each of the rooms had windows with a view of interest; whether it was the lake, the tennis courts or the swimming pool, each scene was quite unique.

"We will have a drink later, but first the boat, so let's get started."

They walked along the jetty and Geoff helped Martin into a small skiff. It felt unstable, and Martin held back.

"Be more gentle, slide in slowly, and once I push you off get your hands on the oars and keep the blades in the water all the time. Feather them, you know; skim them back along the water."

"Why?"

"Because otherwise you will tip the bloody thing up and land in this beautiful lake; you don't want that, old chap, especially with all those nasties in the water."

Geoff pushed off the skiff.

"Wait a minute, Geoff, I've never done this before!" Martin was panicking.

Geoff walked away from the quayside and made his way back to the clubhouse, striding quickly.

"Geoff, wait, come back!"

"Meet you in the bar later, old chap, and remember: keep your oars in the water at all times!"

Martin tried to pull himself together. He rowed and feathered the oars as he pulled them, and the boat moved rapidly through the water. Although he kept his head down to avoid any imbalance, when he looked sideways, he was aware of a multitude of green eyes on the bank not so far away.

He needed to return to the quay as soon as possible, not so much for fun but for his own safety – who would save him if this bloody boat tipped over? He needed to be very careful.

It was getting dark so he kept one oar stationary and retained in the water; the other he paddled carefully and feathered between strokes. The boat turned quickly, but just as he headed for home there was an almighty bellow that shook Martin to his core.

He turned his head to see a pair of hippopotamuses frolicking in the water not more than thirty feet away. It was a crisis and he needed to act accordingly, so with superhuman strength fuelled by panic, he struck the oars solidly into the water and the boat glided through so quickly he rammed the bow into the quay in his quest for safety.

He reached the bar in a fury and did not know whether to drink his first pint of beer or drown de Kok in it.

15

AN ASPIRATION,
JUNE 1980

The challenge of changing his professional duties from work associated with the construction of North Sea oilrigs to the installation of mining products in the middle of Africa appealed to Martin. The challenge was there and he was to work in a continent that had so much to offer but was so backward in producing it.

The climate was second to none and there were so many recreational activities it would spoil him for the future.

He was not proud of the fact that six months ago whilst working in the Shetlands he had informed a member of the security forces that a close friend of his may be operating on behalf of the IRA. He had reasons to believe that this man was plotting to assassinate the British Queen. Although he classed this man a friend he had begun to suspect him after overhearing certain discussions that he was having with a third party.

The MI6 agent involved was George Webster, Martin did not hesitate to report his concerns but had always felt a twinge of guilt in doing so. It seemed that his suspicions were however correct as Barney later disappeared, and a potential terrorist attack was for a time thwarted.

Whatever the situation that now prevailed, Martin felt that he had betrayed Barney, who had been more than an acquaintance at the time. He should have told him face to face rather than report him as if to stab him in the back, but under the circumstances there was nothing else he could have done at the time.

Now in Zambia, he felt like he was a million miles away from Shetland, and he was looking forward to the work ahead of him. This was his bread and butter; it should be fun.

His brief was to control the schedule to ensure that the contractual date was achieved, and costs controlled within the parameters of the budget.

OTHER THAN WORK

From a young boy Martin had had aspirations to become professional in the world of sport. Time had now passed him by as a player but now as an adult and training professional boxers he was hoping for success at the highest level.

Working in Zambia provided him with the raw talent that he wanted to win a world championship; his dream of a real *Rocky* outcome.

During the first few months he reviewed the talent available, discussing their potential with local coaches, and outside of the gym he started to investigate the practicalities of the available local halls that could be suitable for future promotions or utilised for training.

One name mentioned frequently during his research was an ex-boxer called Lemmie Chipili, and Martin wanted to put a face to the name. It seemed that most people knew him as 'the Lion of Kitwe', and his popularity was immense; the man was a living legend. A former heavyweight boxer, after many fights against his African counterparts Lemmie had his chance to fight for the Zambian title held by a white champion. This had the potential to lead to the dismantling of segregation in the world of boxing in Southern Africa.

SETTING UP CAMP

Over the next few weeks Martin was busy setting up the construction site, and during his spare time in the evenings and weekends he worked in the world of boxing and whenever possible he was on the golf course.

The next time he met with Lemmie was at the mine club, and the old boxer was particularly excited. The club had seen better days; it was old and dirty, some doors were almost off their hinges and everything, it seemed, required a coat of paint. Adjacent to the hall was the Diggers Rugby Club; its goalposts were the highest in Africa. Although the hall was in a poor decorative state, it had the potential to make a reasonable boxing hall. Martin noted that the three sides of the hall had wooden terracing that stretched from ground to roof, enough to hold five hundred fans.

The next few weeks saw Martin and Lemmie become firm friends, and they had the hall redesigned to accommodate a gym and change it whenever needed to an indoor stadium.

The smaller back rooms were set up with the appropriate equipment and Martin used one of his on-site contractors to help knock the hall into shape.

In the main hall they drilled four holes into the floor that were used to insert ring posts where ropes were slung; when not in use the ropes were packed away and the holes in the floor capped. Then the place was back to normal, and showed no sign of a training ring ever being there.

Lemmie had been busy. "I have contacted many local boxers and it seems many amateurs want to turn professional with you." He was excited. "They will all come to training tonight, including three of the best amateurs in the country. These are the cream, and all of them are interested in your ideas and the chance to sign professional contracts with you."

"Who is the cream, Lemmie; which one will give us our first world title?"

"Most of them are Olympians and hold medals of one kind or another at amateur level but it is in the stars if any will make professional champions."

That evening in the shabby hall, ten boxers worked out in the converted gymnasium. A strange scenario as the hall was virtually full on two sides, of youngsters who had heard of the event through the grapevine and wanted to see their heroes work out.

One of those observing was a very muscular man of about forty. He wore his trilby hat with its front flipped up in 'Jimmy Durante' style, and once you saw him, you did not forget him.

It was not long before he came down the steps and offered Martin his help. "I will do anything, master – carry the bucket, help with the ring, anything, just say. My name is Benson Chisala, master, and I am here to help you."

"Thank you, Benson; I will ask you should I need help."

Chisala shuffled back up the terrace.

Lemmie laughed. "Benson, Benson."

"Who is he?" asked Martin.

"Oh, he is a guy from the mines who is always showing off his body and his strength to anyone that wants to know."

"Is he a boxer?" Martin asked.

"Not as far as I know, and I have known him for twenty years; nobody knows how old he is, but he's a likeable man."

Little did Martin know at that time that Benson would make a bigger impact in Kitwe than any of the more well-known athletes on the team. He would win hearts with his popularity, topple a dangerous foreign opponent, and fight for fifteen rounds in only his fifth professional fight, only lose the lightweight championship on a split decision.

"The crème de la crème is Francis Musankabala, the bantamweight who is with the skipping rope over there." Lemmie pointed in Musankabala's direction then took a breath and went on. "Favourite to win gold at the Rome Olympics but disqualified for being overweight."

"Overweight?" asked Martin.

"He is a natural featherweight, but the Olympic organisers did not tell him until the initial weigh-in that he was entered as a bantamweight one weight lower then he was. There was a lot of scandal and mouthing off in the press at the time so I think he has had enough of the amateur scene and is now turning to you." He glanced at Martin.

"Then there is no pressure." Martin smiled as he called time for the boxers to wind down.

16

HOME SWEET HOME, 1967—1968

As the morning sun broke through the blinds of Kwasi's rented bedroom he woke up with a start, and looked hard at the empty space in the bed next to him. He was alone, and he felt exposed.

He realised he must stop Naomi before she discussed the situation with his superiors; it would be disastrous for him if he did not, and in no time the whole world would probably know. He must find her quickly!

His first thought was the bus stop; even if she had boarded the bus before he got there, he might still be in time to intercept her further down the road.

He thought for a moment. He had the notion she was still at the school, or perhaps visiting a friend; he was hopeful. One thing was for sure, he needed to talk with her quickly, and he drove fast and furious directly to the campus. Hurrying to the dormitories, he found them already locked up for the holidays. Frustrated, he then headed for the common room; it was also empty, as was the library.

He was starting to panic. Perhaps she had missed the bus? He drove to the stop, but it was deserted; still, he might yet intercept her en route. Checking the timetable, she must have caught the bus at 6.30 – he was now two hours behind it. It was an impossible task to intercept it.

He rang the school caretaker to confirm he hadn't seen her, but there was no answer to his call. Now in a wild panic he then ran towards the bus stop where he may get better information on the bus departure time. On the way he met up with the mineworkers Naomi had encountered earlier that day.

"Why in a rush, my man?" said one of the workers. "Have you missed the bus?"

"No; I needed to give one of my pupils some letters to post before she departed on the bus to Maputo," stammered Kwasi. "Did a tall girl catch the bus?"

"*Nee ek weet nie, omdat daar was baie mensa daar*" [I don't know, because there were too many people there], answered the worker in Afrikaans.

"OK," said Kwasi, who did not understand a word of Afrikaans and got the opinion the man did not want him to understand anyway. He shrugged and hurried on to the phone booth. "Hello, this is Nzema; is that the porter?"

"Yes, it is I, master."

"Have you seen one of my pupils, one Naomi Zimba?"

"No, master, she left yesterday and I have not seen her since."

"Thank you." Kwasi put the phone down.

It was to be six weeks of waiting; a long time for someone with so much guilt and so much to lose.

The old bus jogged along the highway towards Maputo. Its suspension had seen better days and this made it extremely difficult for Naomi, but she had a double seat and made the most of it, sleeping for nearly the whole journey. It seemed to go on forever and she ached from head to foot.

It did not matter: she was going home and could not wait to see her mama and papa, her friends and all the village people. They would throw a welcome-home party, she knew that, and she would need to put on her best face and manners and respect all those who were there. Her father and mother had taught her the meaning of respect; her father had once told her, "Show respect always to every stranger and friend you meet in life, even those who do not show you the same."

From Maputo she flew to Lusaka, and then boarded a bus that was to take her on her last and longest journey for home. After sixteen hours and forty minutes on two buses, a packed flight, then a further bus to Lundazi, she was finally ready to meet her family and friends and it seemed the whole village was there to greet her. Each person waiting would need to be treated equally, as her mother and father had taught her to do.

Naomi followed the protocol and her father's wishes, patiently moving from one villager to the next, each getting a hug. After two hours she went home to the family rondavel, feeling totally exhausted. Her home was a wonderful sight, especially after all she had gone through, and she kissed her mother once more, then collapsed on her bed and was asleep in seconds.

As the days passed she began to feel better and tried to forget the terrible dream that she'd had on her last day of school. She felt alone, desperately wanting to tell her mama everything, but she was too ashamed.

"Naomi, where are you?" Her mama was calling.

"Yes, Mama, I am coming."

She was happy, and gave her mama a huge hug.

"What is that for, my girl?"

"For you, Mama, because I love you. Nothing else."

"There needs to be nothing else, my dear." Hilda put down the laundry she was carrying and returned the hug.

Over the next few days and weeks, Naomi's happiness and confidence grew. She was with family and friends; they lived simply, with little money, but made the most of what they had.

All of this seemed a million miles from the horror at school. It was now a memory, and as the initial pain and embarrassment were left behind she started to feel better and was her usual happy self.

As the holiday dwindled away, she laughed, and ran through the village with her friends, many of whom were new to her. She saw wild animals she'd never thought existed, and stayed awake at night listening to the sounds of the bush, the howls, screeches and bellows. Before going to bed at night she treasured sitting with the elders around an open fire, singing and talking. She met relatives she hadn't known about, all of whom made a fuss of her and told her tales of things long past.

It was during the summer that Naomi celebrated her fifteenth birthday; she did this with the whole village sitting around the campfire, singing and laughing – a glorious memory.

But all things come to an end and it was soon time to leave for her uncle's house in Maputo; he would drive her to Swaziland. The thought of going back to school and facing Kwasi was terrifying, and she dreaded seeing him. How was she to handle the situation, and what if he came on to her again? She did not know how she would react if it happened a second time.

Naomi's father was now village headman, that entailed sitting in court as a comparable Justice of the Peace, and he ruled this domain with a rod of iron. Although he was a strong, silent man, he tried never to favour any one person over another, but he thought this situation could easily change if Naomi came before him; he would be biased. But in any case, he thought, this situation would never occur; she was after all his beloved daughter.

She became a favourite of the village, but all good things come to an end and finally after six weeks Naomi bade a tearful farewell to her home, her friends, her family and her dear mother.

She was to stay at her uncle's home for a few days before he drove her back to school. But it was during this time that she became unwell, and realised her period was late. She was concerned, but did not mention anything to her uncle or aunt and instead prepared for the long journey to Swaziland and school.

Despite her worry regarding the missed periods her life over the next few weeks returned to relative normality, but it wasn't long before her weight increased and her abdomen showed a tell-tale swelling. The reality of the situation hit home and she suspected the worst but, too frightened to ask for help at school, she turned to her mother.

It was not as straightforward as picking up the phone and dialling a number. First she needed permission to use the school phone, and then her call had to be scheduled according to her father's availability in his office back in Lundazi. She phoned during the day and only got through to her mother on the third day's attempt. Naomi cried as she related the situation and they exchanged questions and answers. After putting the phone down Hilda was stunned by the seriousness of the situation, and it was her beloved daughter who was involved.

The elders of the village called a meeting, and it was stormy as the majority of them were still living in the past. The tribal laws were antiquated and they voted for an execution; this not an option in the 1970s. Life had moved on in the community and this type of thing was a rarity; it was especially difficult for the elders to understand modern law in this instance, so, after a long debate into the night, the wise people of the village agreed the matter would be submitted to the urban authorities, and they would decide whether this was to be passed to the criminal courts.

Naomi had a check-up at the local hospital in Swaziland, and it was confirmed that she was pregnant. The situation was now in the hands of the principal, her father and the local authorities. The principal called a meeting to review the situation after he had discussed this with Naomi, and requested that a cross-section of the people involved attend.

Those who attended included her housemistress, Mary (rented house), Chaka, three elders from the village, and a representative from Urban Affairs. The principal also arranged legal representation on an advisory capacity.

Kwasi's name was not mentioned initially. It was expected that he would explain his side of the story in due course, but so far it had not been forthcoming. Now severely tainted, he stayed out of sight and waited for the action that would inevitably follow.

The prevailing situation, if it became common knowledge, might sink the reputation of the school, and as a result the governors were all notified officially.

Naomi remained silent as the village elder representing the headman offered his conclusions. He spoke in a mixture of Lozi and English, the connotations were clear, and the following options passed to the legal representatives:

1. As an immigrant teacher in Swaziland and Zambia, Kwasi Nzema would under ancient tribal law have been sentenced to death for partaking in unlawful intercourse with an underage pupil. As this sentence was now unlikely, it was agreed that a decision on the next step would be made after all the relevant parties had reviewed all of the options. The final decision would be made after the school governors made their recommendation on whether the case should go to the criminal courts.

2. Kwasi would be subject to pay a large compensatory payment to Naomi, and continue to do so until the child became a senior.

3. He would no longer be able to teach children in Swaziland.
4. Naomi would have a final say on the committee's proposals, and she and her parents would have three days after the recommendations have been made to decide how they intended to proceed.

The question of whether it had been seduction or rape was never mentioned, and Kwasi spent three long days waiting for Naomi's decision.

She was distressed throughout the whole procedure, but, after long deliberation, decided her decision would be taken with the best interests of her child in mind. During the trial some discussions were done unofficially between Naomi's family and Kwasi and he suggested that the cleanest way forward and the best thing for the unborn child would be if he proposed marriage to Naomi. This discussion was then put to Naomi and her mother and a decision would be left pending for a few days. He would need to seek employment outside of Swaziland.

Hilda and Naomi's agreed that a marriage would be the best option, it would allow the child to be brought up in a family tradition with an education and better life.

17

FOREVER A CONTRACT?
1968—69

The couple were married in Zambia; a complicated procedure, depending on the wishes of the families involved.

The ancient tribal affair could go on for two or three days. It was a time for celebration in the village, a truly native occasion, colourful, meaningful and a chance for a village party. A church service followed, and this was attended by the Christians in the families and took another two days. Finally, to seal the contract and tie the knot legally, the event was recorded in the archives of the BOME (British Overseas Military Establishment); this served as the town hall in modern Africa but kept its name from the old colonial days.

Naomi gave up her studies to look after her family. It would not have been what her grandfather Angus Peterson would have wanted, but life must go on. Kwasi was transferred to Lusaka and the family was accommodated in a modern bungalow on the university campus.

During the next five years Naomi gave birth to two boys and a girl, but her domestic life was not happy. Kwasi continued his philandering and his conquests did not stop with African girls; it was anybody who would accommodate his needs. He fixed his attentions on a variety of females; one was the wife of an eminent American professor, and he spent most of six months with her whilst her husband was on a degree back in the States. Then he turned his attentions on an Indian widow, then it was a teenager who lasted six months.

This trend continued year in and year out, and most of this time Naomi was pregnant with his children. She opposed his escapades, but in her innocence she was unaware of the alternatives that were available to her, and even if she had known, her financial resources would not have provided her with the means to do anything.

Apart from her unhappy marriage, she had a good circle of friends, both around the campus and within the area's large Ghanaian community. Outside of her husband's infidelity she enjoyed life, although the stigma of his affairs did not leave her.

Every night she waited obediently for Kwasi to come home. She would cook his meals, launder his clothes, and tend to all his needs. Most of the time he never came home at all, and she would empty the dinner she had cooked for him into the bin, then wash his plate and go to bed alone.

Later she moved a daybed into the lounge, and when he did come home she would obediently do whatever he wanted. There was rarely dialogue exchanged between them, and the loneliness was destroying her mentally.

With three lovely children, a nice home and a crooked marriage, she undertook her married life with devout seriousness. She ignored the advice of friends to separate and sue him for divorce; instead she hoped things would change for the better.

With his wide circle of girlfriends it was inevitable that one day Kwasi would meet somebody else, one who would coax him away from married life with Naomi. She was Zambian, much younger than him, and single. At first they kept their association discreet, but as time went by they became more brazen, and it wasn't long before Naomi heard the brutal truth.

18

COMING TO A HEAD, JUNE 1977

The situation came to a head in June 1977. Naomi was at home carrying out household chores, and her mother, who was visiting from Lundazi, was playing with her grandson in his bedroom.

Then Naomi heard a loud knock on the door and answered it to find a young woman of about twenty standing outside. Her visitor did not start with the preliminaries, nor offer the remotest of introductions, but went straight into a tirade of aggression. Her voice was raised as she spoke to Naomi in Bemba.

"I have been in love with Kwasi for two years. We intend to get married after he divorces you, and it is now time that you move out of this house and let us live here."

"It is in this house where I live with Kwasi as my husband, and our children," Naomi explained politely.

"But you must go now. We will look after the children; we are together."

"What are you talking about? Are you mad?"

"I am not mad, and you are not wanted – just go!"

Her voice was high, loud and threatening. The disturbance stirred the neighbours, and already a group of women were gathering in the road nearby.

Naomi's face showed no emotion but gracefully she beckoned the girl to come in, then stood back to allow her to enter the house.

The girl looked straight ahead; not a glance in Naomi's direction, only a faint smile, as though in triumph.

It was a mistake. The first blow stunned her; the next was a clenched fist that hit her around the temple, and she was felled in an instant.

The girl lay motionless on the floor, and an eerie silence came over the house; Naomi did not say or do anything to assist the woman on the floor. After a few minutes their was a sign of life, it came from her right leg, which somehow hung just off the floor, it started to oscillating slightly as though treading water.

The house remained silent, with no other movement apart from that of a fly whose wings were moving so fast they could have been applauding the action.

A few more seconds, and the silence was broken by a gasp from the girl. Naomi bent down, grabbed her by the hair, dragged her screaming to the bathroom, dunked her head in the toilet bowl and flushed.

Hearing the commotion, Hilda picked up her grandson, laid him on the bed and ran to see what was happening. At the sight of the stricken girl she screamed, "Naomi! What have you done? Who is this girl?"

A woman's rage has no equal. Naomi pushed the girl's head into the toilet, and flushed once more. The girl tried to scream, but any noise was drowned out. Hilda, afraid of what Naomi might do next, put her arms around her daughter and guided her to the bedroom.

Soon the group of neighbour women were just outside the house. They waited until the wailing stopped, then entered to find the girl sitting on the bathroom floor, exhausted, her elbow still resting on the toilet.

In the bedroom Naomi was crying shamelessly in her mother's arms. It was the sound of a woman alone in the world, without husband or children, humiliated and discarded.

The neighbours listened as her mother related the situation; it must have been interesting as they all settled on the floor. After Hilda had finished, the group had a full understanding of the situation and turned on the girl, hustling her from the house and jeering as she stumbled into the road, wet and ashamed. Kwasi wisely stayed away, and hoped things would settle before he returned to explain things in a more civilised manner.

Hilda travelled home to Lundazi and Naomi busied herself with the children. The neighbours kept their distance and the situation eased. Kwasi returned as if nothing had happened and became more attentive to the family than he had been in years; he was forthcoming, talkative, and helped with whatever he could to show willing.

This situation prevailed for a few weeks, until one day in August Kwasi advised Naomi that he would take the children to Ghana during October and November to visit his family. "It is two years since they last saw my family and they have not had a chance to spoil our new son, so we will travel in a couple of days."

Naomi agreed and the family flew to Accra and booked into a hotel. Everything seemed normal at first, so she decided to book an appointment at the hotel's hairdressing salon.

While she was separated from her children, Kwasi made his move and packed them into the hired car. It was over two hours later that he returned to collect Naomi from the salon. "My mother has taken the children to the homelands to visit their grandmother, so I will stay and bring them home next week. You will return to Swaziland tomorrow and I will join you with the children in two weeks from now."

Naomi raised her voice. "This was not the arrangement, Kwasi; I want to be with them."

"They have come to see my family, and my family will have more freedom with them if you are not there. Don't worry they will be fine. I will take you to the airport as planned tomorrow."

"No, I will stay and they will travel with me." Naomi was firm.

"That is impossible. Do you want to stay here in the hotel for another week alone?"

She glared at him for many minutes. "If they are not back in a week, I will make your life hell."

"I will pick you up tomorrow, say, nine?" And he walked quickly away from the hotel.

She returned to Zambia feeling lonely, desolate and betrayed.

Two weeks passed, and Naomi answered a knock on the door.

"I am the facilities officer at the university." The man handed her a letter.

"What is this?"

"It is to inform you that Mr Nzema has resigned," he advised.

"What do you mean, resigned?" Naomi was in shock.

"Ma'am, I only do what I am told. The university had received his resignation letter and as a result you must leave the house."

She tried to collect her thoughts. Where was she to go? What was she to do? Her children, her beloved children, where were they?

19

NEVER JUDGE A FRIEND BY THEIR PASTIMES, 1977—80

The week passed quickly but Naomi made little progress in finding alternative accommodation or a job. She had no money.

On her last day in the house, she was alone and feeling totally desperate. Then she received a telephone call from an old friend.

"Naomi, my darling, I am sorry to hear about your man Kwasi; I understand that he has flown the nest. What are your plans?"

Naomi was in a very sombre mood. Normally a positive and bright person, the recent events had left her feeling low. She did not trust anyone in the first instance, but waited until she understood the terms of the call.

"Hi, Pet, I am glad to hear from you. To answer your question, I have no plans at the moment; it is my last day in our university accommodation and if I do not find a place to live independently, I will accept the offer from the Ghanaian community. It is their way of apologising for Kwasi's fun and games, but I would rather not take it; I feel they would be watching me all the time and reporting back to him."

"Come stay with me, my child; we have a spare room and you can stay as long as you want."

"Thank you, Pet, that will be nice. I really appreciate your offer, and would certainly like to take you up on it; that is, once I arrange for storage of my belongings. I will book a taxi."

"Nonsense," said Petula Partington. "Jim will come and pick you up immediately, once you are ready."

Petula was a good type, although Naomi thought that she had some dubious friends; she was a little older than Naomi, and more worldly, with a broader experience of life and love. Married to a white expatriate working in the mines, they lived close to the main town of Kitwe. Her house was standard, supplied by the mines as a term of contract, but with a woman's touch and a man's ingenuity it made an impeccable family home.

Jim had two teenage daughters. They lived in England with their mother, but during school holidays they came to Zambia and stayed with him and Pet. The couple did not have children together, Jim having already had a vasectomy before he met his second wife. She often spent time away from him, moving in the circles of emerald smugglers and prostitutes, and the local gossip among the expatriate community was that she was more than loosely linked to both. Nevertheless, they were a welcoming couple, warm, hospitable and, in Naomi's case, very loyal.

Naomi continued to look for work, it was a tedious task, every day writing and phoning companies and people who thought they could help her., but life was not easy and jobs were hard to find. Although young, vibrant and intelligent, it was difficult for her to get work without experience, but she would not take no for an answer and continued to pursue any rumour of vacancies that she picked up from the media or her friends. Her money had dried up and the little she'd made from selling the marital home's furniture was now gone.

There was no word from Kwasi or the children, and the Ghanaian community she often visited were not saying anything about him even if they knew. Without her children close to her she felt despair and a loneliness she had never experienced before; if it had not been for her friends, life would have been unbearable.

Then, quite out of the blue, she heard of a vacancy as a receptionist at the Mindolo Institute of Education. It was an educational foundation that had been set up by a church trust and included all aspects of training and education. She hurried to complete the application form and took it to the institute in person.

It seemed the interview went well, as the next day she received a letter offering her the position and started work almost immediately. She was especially happy with the situation as the job provided accommodation and lunch, this would mean moving out of the Partington household and she would miss their hospitality but it would give her own space.

The majority of students at the institute came from Zambia, but others were from far and wide, although all were associated with the church. Naomi liked mixing and talking with the students; her work was associated with organising their travel and accommodation. There were also activities that included interacting with other campuses; this gave her the opportunity to discuss her situation with the resident teachers and students in her quest to find her children.

Her life was active during the working day but the evenings were lonely. She just hoped someone would give her the information she so desperately wanted.

The weekends were a fun time for her and she often managed to visit her friends in Kitwe. This situation particularly suited Pet when her husband was working night shifts. Naomi continued to visit the Ghanaian community in the hope of news of her children, but the Ghanaians remained non-committal.

When visiting Pet on one occasion, she noticed a man walking away from her friend's house. He looked awkward, as if he was trying not to be noticed. An uncouth sort of fellow, from his appearance he looked more West African than local. Naomi was sure that he was not a hired help, and she was relieved when she found her friend safe and sound.

"Was that Jim's supervisor I saw? His foreman, perhaps?" Naomi was inquisitive.

"What foreman? What man?" answered Pet.

"The man I saw coming from the back of your house."

"Oh, him – no, he was just a salesman trying to sell me the green stuff" (emeralds), Pet informed her.

Naomi wasn't satisfied, and waited patiently. "He didn't look Zambian, nor was he carrying anything. Are you sure you haven't a secret boyfriend?" she joked.

Pet giggled and looked at Naomi inquisitively. "Have you any money, Naomi?" she asked, turning their conversation on its head.

"You know I have little money left after stoppages; why do you ask?" Naomi was confused.

"You could make money easily," said Pet. "We could just ask some guys around and they will give us money – obviously it will need to be whilst Jim is at work." She chuckled, and waited for an answer.

"And what do they expect in return?" Naomi glared at her friend.

"Oh, come, dear Naomi," Pet said, puckering her lips. "Just a kiss, and if it's anything more they pay big time."

There was silence, and Naomi moved out to the kitchen. "What time is Jim home?" she shouted. "Because it's time you peeled the potatoes."

Nothing more was said between them, either about the man or about the duties that Pet implied she'd performed for him.

As the months went by Naomi withdrew into her shell and became an introvert. She lost her joy, and the jogging she had started at Petula's house was a thing of the past, and her visits to her friend slowly diminished. Her mission to find her children was now an obsession, her own personal tragedy.

During her visits to the Partington household, she met and became friends with a girl who also visited them. Her name was Veronica and she was about Naomi's age, and worked in Kitwe as a secretary. A pretty and happy individual, she had sympathy for Naomi's situation.

"Perhaps tomorrow you will hear something, dear Naomi," she would say, but as tomorrow came, and the next day, and the next, nothing!

Naomi found comfort in the young secretary because she too had a problem, and it was reassuring for Naomi to know that other people also had their cross to bear, sometimes much worse than her own.

Veronica came from the west of Zambia and a tribe called the Lozi. She was bright at school and learned quickly, and was soon promoted from secondary school to Pitman's Secretarial College, and into the big towns where she worked for the Highways Department in local government. Her education had taken place in a small but select school; it was outback country and life was still traditional there. Family tradition in Africa meant strict morals, honesty, integrity and a basic living.

So coming to town, life was a big surprise for her; she rode in large cars, attended noisy discos, was continually approached by boys, and could never make ends meet where money was concerned. Life in the big mining towns was different than in her village; it was faster, more expensive, and money needed to be budgeted. She found it difficult to do this at first but was learning fast.

However, her life became even more complicated when the headman of her village arranged her marriage to an older local man.

This situation was unexpected; she had progressed from village tradition and was enjoying the new ways of the city and its people. But the village was not the same: it upheld its old traditions and her parents shared those beliefs. They approved of the man who had been proposed and influenced Veronica to comply with their tribal principles, and she finally succumbed.

They were married in the traditional way in the village. Veronica's husband, John Mivila, was a successful businessman who originated from the village, and made his money from retail. At first they lived in her flat in town, with him travelling back to the village on business, but after a time he tried to persuade Veronica to return with him and live there permanently. It was after a few months of playing a part-time 'custom wife' that Veronica brought things to a head.

"John, it is time we were married properly," she said.

"Sure, Veronica, we are married," he assured her.

"No, John, I want a BOMA wedding – you know, official."

There was silence and John walked towards the door, explaining he had a business appointment.

"Another thing," she cried after him. "If we are married then we live together, not just on a Monday, Tuesday and sometimes Saturday."

The door slammed, and Veronica was alone again.

A week later she received a note from John:

My dearest Veronica,

I am writing to tell you how much I love you.

My feelings are so intense I want you to move into my home and we can live as a family with my first wife and two children. I have told her we will live together and she is happy with this situation.

On Saturday we will go to the Nkana cinema, then return home for supper and the family can discuss the situation.
Looking forward to seeing you.

Yours forever,
John

Veronica did not wait for Saturday, but packed her bags and jumped on the first bus west to stay with her brother. She cried the whole way, and after some serious discussions with the rest of her family they decided that she should return with her brother and confront her husband.

It was exactly two weeks later that she, her brother and the village headman met in the community hut and the situation was resolved. Veronica and John would be divorced in due course, but in the meantime she would start a new life in the town of Kitwe.

20

A TIME TO REFLECT

Naomi cried after Veronica explained the impossible conflict between tradition and the new, faster life of the twentieth century. It seemed from her experience that the African man would utilise the traditional African life to suit his male ego, without regarding the woman's wishes.

Naomi was convinced that John had tried to use and manipulate Veronica just to suit himself. It seemed that the African man was born to deceive and be unfaithful.

Jim Partington worked hard as a supervisor for a small contractor fabricating and erecting tanks for the mines. He was a rotund character who enjoyed his life with Pet; his social life was limited, although he did play golf. Otherwise he barely ventured outside his pretty bungalow. On one of the few occasions he did go out, it was on a company social booze-up, which was also held at the golf club.

It was on this occasion that he met and became friendly with an Irishman called Brendan Keogh. He was a single man who had been living in Zambia for five years and worked as the manager of a foundry in the Kitwe area. Small and chirpy, he was also immensely strong, probably after many years lifting heavy forgings whilst working in the foundry, and was popular with the other expats at the golf club. His humour was dry and he would do anything to draw a smile from the people he kept company with.

As he was based in Kitwe, it was not long before Jim invited Brendan to his home. His humour was tested at the Partington household following his introduction to the three women; all, it seemed, were suffering from pre-menstrual stress. Naomi seemed to be forever moping and grieving over her missing children, Veronica was perturbed about being used by her man, and Petula was concerned about the drop in the price of emeralds. Brendan fitted into the group immediately, even though the women outnumbered him and Jim. His humour was not wasted on the others, especially with its light sexual connotations.

It wasn't long before he struck up a friendship with Veronica. Their association developed quickly and they soon found a way to live together either at her place or his. Life got even better for them both when Veronica found a job in Kitwe, close to where her new boyfriend worked; it was a bonus, and they made the most of the change.

Naomi always managed to attend when the Partingtons threw a party. Her unhappiness was plain to see, although she never complained about her situation, and those around her always showed kindness. She became an enigma, always arriving and leaving parties alone, dancing by herself and never holding a conversation with anyone longer then a few minutes; when she did dance alone her style was exotic it tended to transfix those who watched her. It was a cross between Pilates and Arabic belly dance: she proved to be quite a cabaret, everyone clapping enthusiastically when she finished.

Although generally unhappy, she always appeared to enjoy herself at the parties; they took her away from the unhappiness of her everyday life, and with her eyes shut she transcended into another world. It was as if she was in a cocoon; her body pulsated rhythmically with the music, sometimes appearing to be static, whilst at other times vibrations shuddered through her.

Her hands, large and beautifully shaped, artistically manipulated the rhythm with grace and flamboyance.

Veronica and Petula were sympathetic to Naomi's loneliness; however as a single person she created an uncomfortable atmosphere within the group, especially when the men talked to her with more intent than they did with their partners. She needed someone, it would keep her mind occupied, and it would comply fully with the other females.

They persuaded Brendan and Jim to look out for a potential mate for her. But when the subject was mentioned to Naomi, she flew into a rage: "I do not want a man, they are users; my love is for my children and only my children."

The others soon realised that this subject should not be raised again. But despite her attitude, her friends continued to keep a lookout for a suitable partner for her. He would need to be supportive, understanding and sympathetic to Naomi's needs.

It was the end of the day, the sun had set and the sky was a brilliant red. The bush below looked dark and mysterious as the four drank cocktails on the veranda, enjoying a spectacular evening, the likes of which they had seen many times before.

Brendan was staring into space, Veronica's head cradled in his lap. He suddenly perked up. "Jim, lad, if there's not someone up at the golf course who can give that Naomi a big kiss and make her forget her troubles just for a moment, then I'm a Welsh leprechaun."

Jim didn't look up, but grinned, nodding in agreement.

Veronica lifted her head slightly from Brendan's lap. "Today I visited town with Naomi. It was really nice: we shopped, we walked and laughed, it gave us fresh air and exercise; then when I went into a shop I left Naomi outside and she met someone."

"Met someone – who?" The other three were all ears.

"I am not sure who he was.

"A man approached Naomi and opened the conversation. He said, 'Don't I know you from somewhere, dear?'

"She quickly looked to see who owned this educated voice. 'Maybe you do. Perhaps from the Mindolo Institute, as I work there,' she answered.

"'Yes, that is at the Economics Foundation; you are the receptionist and I remember you very well. My name is James Khakkeki.'

"Naomi took a closer look at the man. He was perhaps forty, and yes, she did remember him; he was something to do with Shell or some other company. Although he was balding slightly, he was elegant.

"'Look, my dear, when is your day off? Perhaps we can go for a drive?'

"Naomi stalled. 'I am busy until next Monday; I don't know.' She tried to put him off.

"'It's been a pleasure meeting you,' said Khakkeki. 'I'll see you a week on Tuesday and I will not take no for an answer.' And he was gone as quickly as he arrived."

Naomi pushed the situation to the back of her mind, and forgot about him until she saw him drive up to her accommodation the following Tuesday. She panicked and ran to the bathroom. The bell rang in her small flat and, still in her dressing gown, she half-opened the door.

"Hello, my dear. Would you care to come for a drive to Luanshya? I have business there; then perhaps we can have a meal in the mine restaurant."

The Luanshya mine mess was perhaps the best eating house in Zambia, and the thought appealed to Naomi as she hadn't eaten for two days, having overspent her allowance.

"Wait for me in your car, please, Mr Khakkeki; I will be just ten minutes."

The two-litre super saloon purred along the road west from Kitwe, and Naomi and James Khakkeki sat in silence. She thought of her youngest son, who'd been two when she'd last seen him, and still in recovery after a heart operation performed by Dr Christian Barnard in South Africa. He was a fragile young boy, but because of his predicament attracted a special devotion and had been spoilt as a result of all the attention his family thrust upon him.

A tear ran down her cheek, and she tried to change her train of thought, but then she suddenly became aware of where she was going and it jerked her into reality. "Where are you going, Mr Khakkeki? This is not the road to Luanshya."

"Don't worry, Naomi; I have some business in Ndola first and this is the shortest way there – it will save us time and money. If we are delayed due to my business interests we can stay at the Naoma Lodge which is situated between the two towns, then travel back first thing in the morning."

Oh my God. Naomi was in a panic. *I am to be used again,* she thought, *by a man who wants his way and doesn't give a thought to what I want.*

They remained in silence for the next hour until a few small white houses came into view. Khakkeki turned left, swinging the car right into a government-style building, then switched off the engine and got out.

"I will not be long; please be patient."

Naomi sat staring out at a large evergreen hedge. She asked herself what she was doing in the middle of nowhere with a man she hardly knew; she should have stayed at home. He seemed nice and looked respectable, obviously well connected, probably financially comfortable, but almost certainly had a wife and children at home.

Her mind raced, and she reviewed her options. Should she get out of the car now and walk, stay and demand a ride back to Kitwe, or stay with him in the lodge? Walking was out of the question – a young woman walking alone was just too dangerous, with rape, robbery and death all possibilities. She shuddered. She could demand a ride back to Kitwe, but if this was the case and it was brought to the notice of the Mindolo Institute she could loose her job. *If the story got about in the campus everyone would think that I am a stupid person.* If she stayed with him he probably would demand sex and what if she resisted and a struggle occurred anything could happen she started to cry. *Oh God. Please help me!* Naomi's mind whirled. What if she became pregnant? She had not been on the pill for two years. She suddenly thought it best to escape from the car and obtain a lift from a passer-by. She fumbled with the door catch but found it difficult to open. Everything she tried was unsuccessful, but eventually she opened the window, stretched her head out into the warm air and located the outside door latch. The door opened, and she put her long leg onto the tarmac.

A voice startled her. "How silly of me not to tell you where to powder your nose. Come, my girl, follow me." Khakkeki held her arm, escorting her into the building. "It's through the swing doors and immediately left," he said. "I will wait in the car." And he left her.

She pushed her way into the toilet, trying to think of an excuse to make him take her home. She could shame him, but the police were out of the question; an investigation would blight her and she would almost certainly lose her job.

Why had she accepted this date with a man she did not know? She was in a perilous situation. If she did submit to him she could become pregnant, and what of venereal disease or even HIV? She was beside herself.

She stood up from the toilet seat and pulled the door open, their were two large African women talking, one had a baby in a shawl that was wrapped around her back, their was not much room so she gently edged past them and walked from the building. She found the car empty. It was open, and she got back into her seat. The situation took her aback; everything was silent. He was nowhere to be seen, damn him. She opened the car door and slid outside again, looking around, but she was alone.

Then Khakkeki appeared as if from nowhere. "Look, my dear, it's getting dark, and with the road as dangerous as it is, I have made arrangements with the local hotel for the night."

Naomi said nothing, and the brave face she had put on a few minutes earlier deserted her. She made her retreat and could only think of a way to minimise the obvious.

21

AN EXPERIENCE
BEST FORGOTTEN,

The hotel was small but clean, and the room sparsely furnished. Khakkeki followed Naomi inside, and she suddenly turned to him. "James, I need to explain that I have three children, and I feel that this is a mistake." She pleaded with him. "I have a young child at home and he is sick."

"But, my dear, you didn't mention this before, and it is too dangerous to go home now, and by the way did you mention that you have two girls as neighbours, can't they look after the child ?" He seemed genuinely concerned, and she softened.

"Thet are too young!" Naomi said dejectedly, then blurted out, "This situation is a mistake. I do not want to share this bed with you, and I want to go home tonight."

Khakkeki smiled warmly. "Who said anything about sharing a bed?" He put his hand gently on her shoulder.

Naomi glanced at him.

"Look, Naomi, I am going to step out for a short while; I have some local business. Please bolt the door and get some rest; we will talk when I get back." He smiled down at her. "Please be ready for me when I get back. I will not be long, and don't worry, I will take precautions." With that he moved swiftly to the door and disappeared outside.

Naomi was alone, and a black emptiness came over her as she lay down on the bed with her eyes open, her thoughts scattered.

Suddenly she was with her children again; everyone was laughing, and they were throwing a ball from one to another. The youngest boy was strapped into a small pushchair but was clapping his long, thin hands in unison with his brother and sister, who were singing an African song.

The spell was broken. It seemed only minutes since Khakkeki had left the room, when there were shouts outside the hotel, then gunshots. Her dream was shattered.

She froze and listened. There was calm, and then she jumped in fear at a loud knocking on the door. At first it was intermittent, but soon it became louder and more frenzied.

"Naomi, Naomi – be quick, it's me, Khakkeki."

Immediately she had unlocked the door, Khakkeki pushed into the room and collapsed; she saw blood spreading across the wooden floor. Feeling sick, she put her fist in her mouth to hold back a scream. Khakkeki moaned, and she bent down to see what she could do for him.

"Go, my dear, get out quickly; they will kill you." He spluttered more blood. "Take this and go now, hide in the bush, but get out." His blood-stained hand held a leather tag with writing and a code number was stapled to it. "Go now!"

Frightened, she left the room and ran down the stairs; at the bottom there was a fire door which she kicked open and ran from the hotel, heading for the nearest bush. She was familiar with the environment from her home village, and knew how to survive in it. Stopping briefly, she broke a branch from a nearby tree and with the leaves brushed over her tracks, disguising the trail.

In the bush she kept her eyes open, carefully picked out her route and edged along a path, moving away from the hotel as quickly as she could. She moved stealthily, moving the stick in front of her to distract any snakes or nasties that were present. She knew that snakes have poor eyesight, and will strike at the first thing that moves. After maintaining a slow rate of progress, she was scared and her hands were shaking, her top lip trembling, she stopped and took stock of her position and the safest way to get away without detection.

She had no way of knowing if those who had hurt Khakkeki were aware of her existence; they would probably have guessed, if they had gone to the room after she'd left, that someone had been with him. She had left personal items on the bed; if they found them and not the tag with the code number it was certain that they would try to find her.

Cold, hungry and scared, she used all her know-how to find a way home through the bush. She was relying on her own intuition, and hoped it had not deserted her.

It was the first time in her life that she had needed to use the bush tactics her family had taught her. They were helping her survive now, but it was one thing to be trained in something and another to put it into practice.

After zigzagging through the terrain for miles she reached a small road. It was well maintained, the tarmac fresh and the surface frequently used. She checked her position with the moon and stars and headed in the direction of Ndola, keeping close to the edge of the road to avoid drunk drivers and being discovered by the wrong people. She passed some village people along the way; each gave her greetings and she replied in their tongue so as not to arouse suspicion.

Her mind played tricks, and she became confused. She visualised her junior school in Lundazi; she thought of her old school friends and wondered what they were all doing now. After a time her mind cleared and she realised she had been walking for nearly four hours.

Turning a bend, she met with a junction that intersected with a much larger road, and guessed it was the main connection between Ndola and Kitwe. She continued to walk as quickly as possible, her bare feet cool on the tarmac, but before she even noticed it was there an old bakkie stopped beside her.

An elderly man was struggling with the gear stick, and shouted, "Do you want a lift to Kitwe?" Once he crunched it into gear, he followed up: "If you do then jump in the back quickly, and I will be on my way." She did not want a second offer and leapt into the back; there were a number of elderly women already sitting there and she assumed they were travelling to the fields for work.

The bakkie dropped her off in Kitwe and she walked quickly to her small accommodation at the institute. Her hands were still shaking, there was perspiration on her brow, her life was again in turmoil, and what had happened to Khakkeki? Who had done this to him, and why?

She looked at the note to see if she could ascertain anything from the numbers. It was hopeless; she did not have a clue, and to inform the police would draw too much attention to the Mindolo Institute. If it became known that she was involved with anything underhand going on, the governors would certainly dismiss her, which was the last thing she wanted. And what about this wretched number – what did it mean?

She picked up the phone. "Petula, is that you?"

"Yes, my dear, what can I do for you?"

"Do you know a man called Khakkeki?"

"I know a few men by that name, my dear, what does he look like?"

"He is a big man, very expensively dressed, and he took me against my will to a hotel." Naomi was breathless.

"That is nothing extraordinary," said Pet.

Naomi continued. "But he went out just as we arrived and came back after an hour with blood all over him."

There was silence at the other end of the line, then Petula asked, "Who knows about this, and how did you get home? Were you pursued?"

"I don't think so, but he gave me a paper with a number on it before he passed out. I think he died, there was so much blood."

"Have you told the police?" asked Pet.

"No, should I?" Naomi waited for a reply.

"Do not do anything, do not speak with anyone about this until I return your call, do you understand?"

"Yes, thank you, Pet."

The line went dead.

Naomi had calmed down and now her situation simply felt surreal. Relaxed, she went to work as though nothing had happened and the day passed quickly.

At eight o'clock that evening the phone rang. "Naomi, I have some news. Your man Khakkeki survived and is in hospital in Ndola."

"Do I need to tell the police?" asked Naomi.

"No, he does not want any interference."

"What was it all about?" Naomi dared not ask too many questions as it seemed Pet knew all the answers.

"Naomi, forget him, for he is a dealer, a fraudster and a money launderer. Do not get involved, and forget you have seen him – if you meet again, excuse yourself and walk away."

"What about this number I have?"

"It's probably a bank account, so pass it to me and I will ensure that it is returned to him. Is that clear? Forget that this has happened."

"Thank you, Petula, you are a true friend."

"I don't know about that, but let's move on; it could have been dangerous for you."

The call was ended.

Naomi always felt better after visiting her friends Pet and Jim. Although she did not agree with Pet's infidelity, she found her a good and loyal friend.

It was Friday and the institute's director informed Naomi that her working week would change; she would now be required to work on Saturday and Sunday. This was due to the new students' enrolment period before their Monday start.

22

CURFEW, SEPTEMBER 1981

In 1964 Zambia became the ninth African state to win independence, and Kenneth Kaunda became their first president.

He was born in 1924 to Malawian parents, a teacher by profession, as was his Presbyterian father. As in many African countries, after independence the governing of Zambia was never going to be easy, and his time in office was plagued by tribalism, unrest and civil war.

Many African state leaders who sought independence from the British formed a group and called themselves the African National Congress, a movement that was to achieve independence from the British in the majority of African countries, but this did not happen without sacrifice and some, including Kenneth Kaunda, demonstrated so vigorously that they were subsequently detained in prison by the British for long periods of time. When those who did experience incarceration were released they gained hero status, as did Kaunda when he was finally released in 1960.

During his time as president ethnic unrest was prevalent, and in an effort to stabilise this, Kaunda imposed a curfew on the country, forbidding any movement outside the home between six o'clock in the evening and six in the morning. His party announced that any person found on the streets between these times would be deemed an agitator and imprisoned without recourse.

At Jim and Pet's house, weekend curfews were a good reason to party, and the group made the most of the situation. On most Saturdays the house was full of friends, with parties continuing through the night until the curfew was lifted at six the next day.

On one particular weekend Pet was looking as glamorous as usual when Naomi arrived at five o'clock on Friday evening. Jim was his usual untidy self – he was cooking meat on the braai. It was sizzling and he occasionally poured beer over it to stop it burning; he said it would give it a better flavour.

Brendan and Veronica arrived shortly afterwards and the group started the weekend as they intended to finish it. The three ladies went into the house whilst Jim and Brendan talked outside. The night was warm and the sky clear.

"You know, Jim, last week I played golf with another Irishman who has just moved to the area. He is called Charles Siddons, hell of a nice guy. I have invited him over tonight; being Irish like myself, he can charm Naomi with his incessant talking and good humour."

"Does she know yet?" asked Jim.

"No, and she won't until he arrives."

"What does he do?" asked Jim. "For work, I mean."

"Nothing at the moment, although he told me he's trained as a mechanic and worked on some site somewhere in the UK. I hope Naomi doesn't throw a tantrum when she meets him."

Jim laughed. "Even if she does, there is no place for her to go once the curfew starts." He was uneasy in case of any misunderstanding.

"That's right, but let's advise her that we have a golfing friend coming tonight; nothing obvious." Brendan looked mischievous.

"Naomi?" Jim shouted towards the house.

"Yes, Jim?" It was Naomi's heavily accented Afrikaans tone. "Brendan wants you a moment."

A few seconds passed and Naomi skipped into the garden, her head held high. She was in a good mood, it seemed. Towering above a much smaller Brendan, she smiled down on him. "Did you want something, Brendan?"

"Yes, my dear – I have invited a friend over tonight; his name is Charles Siddons. He is Irish and alone in Zambia, so please be nice to him. There is no hidden significance to my inviting him; he is our friend."

"Who is this Charles Siddons?" Naomi quizzed. "Is he sixty years old, with white hair?" She was going to add, 'and a fat stomach', but looked at Jim's before saying anything more.

"No, he is the same age as me," Brendan said. He waited for a few moments and then added, "That's old, I suppose." There was silence, and he continued, "But he is a kind man and lots of fun."

Naomi hesitated, and her thoughts made her more defensive. *A* makiwa *[white man], youngish, is coming tonight. It sounds suspicious to me*, she thought. She looked down at Brendan with her deep brown eyes. "Please make it clear to your Mr Siddons that he can find better girls in the bush, who are younger and prettier than me." She turned angrily, as if offended by their suggestion.

"But we are not suggesting an association between the two of you; only that you welcome him."

"That I will do willingly, but that is all. Your man can look elsewhere." She headed for the bathroom, her head held high, but her heart low.

"I only tried." Brendan's rich voice sounded disappointed, and Jim continued to look at the floor. He felt embarrassed.

The kitchen door swung open and Veronica burst in. "What have you done to that poor girl, talking about this Mr Goodwill, an Englishman without a woman?"

She turned towards the bathroom, but stopped when she heard Brendan's voice. "Veronica," he began, "it is Mr Siddons, not Mr Goodwill, and he's not English at all – he's like me, Irish."

She didn't look round, but smiled and shouted, "Then, Mr Keyhole, he can't be all bad, I suppose."

"What can you do with them?" said Brendan, and Jim nodded.

"What time is he due here tonight? It's only five minutes before the curfew is due to start."

"OK, don't worry." Brendan's eyes went to the ceiling.

It was ten minutes past six when the doorbell shrilled.

"Someone at the door," laughed Pet. "Hello, Charles, it is so nice to meet you." She was at her most charming as she invited the Irishman into the house.

"Where are they?" asked Charles.

"Oh, they are outside as usual drinking beer, but before you go out, can I introduce you to someone?"

"Of course, and who might that be?"

23

NOTHING LIKE SEEING OLD FRIENDS, NOVEMBER 1981

The Nkana Golf Course is positioned on the outskirts of Kitwe. Leading to the clubhouse from the main road is a two-kilometre access road; it is narrow with a few nasty bends, and not something for a golfer to look forward to after a tiring round and a few strong drinks. The access road normally does not present a problem to the driver on his way in to play a round, it is on exit where the problem exists. It can be an utmost challenge for the unprepared driver, especially a slightly inebriated one; according to Geoff de Kok, one can take all the bends at sixty miles per hour and enjoy the ride at the same time. Along the winding route there are many trees, and these are a welcome break from the sun that burns incessantly in the hot season.

Brendan had driven this route so many times, in various states of inebriation, that he often boasted that he was getting better and faster after each trip. Today it was his turn to drive, and in the car with him were Jim and de Kok's replacement Martin Valeron, who had joined the group on an invitation from Brendan. The two had met a few days earlier at the club.

Brendan slowed to a stop just outside the car park and allowed Martin to practise his swing on the range before parking nearer to the club.

"I hope he gets on well with his new partner, this guy Siddons – and by the way, is that name Irish?" asked Jim.

"To be sure, it is not, but then he is probably from the English side – you know, the Black North. But it doesn't matter; I am sure they will get on fine."

At the clubhouse, they changed their shoes and shared a locker to store the clothes they'd need after a shower later.

The bar was big, with the viewing area built at thirty degrees to the fairway, providing a good view of the eighteenth green. Charles had not arrived when they entered the bar, so with twenty minutes to spare, they ordered drinks from the waiter.

After a few minutes Brendan perked up. "Well, here comes our man. Good morning, Charles, glad you could make it."

Martin, on seeing the man he knew as Barney Coughlin, was struck dumb. He went pale, fidgeted for a few minutes and then held out his hand. "Hi, er, Charles; long time no see." He sat down, embarrassed that he knew the man's secret, and averted his eyes. "You did say your name was Charles, didn't you?"

"It is."

Brendan noticed the panic on Martin's face. "Have you met before?"

Charles turned to Brendan – "How are you, Paddy?" – and then looked at Martin. He did not show surprise or fear. "So, you must be my new partner. That's great, and it's nice to meet you."

"Likewise." Martin sat down without another word and forced a smile.

The others, sensing a tense situation, also found seats. The waiter put the tray on the table, and said, in his deep African accent, "I took the liberty and brought four of everything; I hope that is what you want?"

"Of course, John, that is wonderful, and make sure you put this on my account. And here is something for you." He squeezed some notes into the waiter's hand.

FOUR HOURS LATER

"I knew it would be a good game, and sorry that the local boys beat the newcomers." Brendan joked with Jim, and looked mischievously at Martin and Charles.

"It was good company, but I played lousy." Charles smiled as he patted Martin on the back.

"Thanks, old man, but don't worry; I played badly too. There is always another time."

"Let's order some cold drinks before I collapse in this heat, and then we can shower and have a few more," Brendan laughed.

In unison, they all said, "Absolutely", but it turned out to be more than just one drink; it was a few before Brendan headed off to the shower, followed minutes later by Jim.

Martin and Charles continued sipping their drinks. Charles grimaced and looked sheepishly at his old friend. "I knew that you had come to Africa but did not expect you to be here. Nevertheless, it is good to see you." He rose to leave for the shower, but then gripped Martin's forearm and whispered, "Please do not say anything to my friends. I will explain everything whenever we can get together; is that all right with you?"

"This is the strangest reunion I have ever had, and if it is a coincidence then the chances of it occurring must be incredible, but yes, that's fine," Martin laughed. "Let's meet next week. Ring me at the office and we will make a plan, and don't worry, I will not say a word to anyone in the meantime." He held out his hand to Charles and they shared a firm handshake.

Ironically, he had only recently spoken with George Webster, but now with Barney (or Charles) turning up, things were different. Next time he might have to tell him the news. He thought for a moment. *No – let the man have his say and we may even let sleeping dogs lie.* Either that or when George called he could just not answer the phone.

Arriving back at his house, Martin threw his laundry into the basket, poured himself a glass of water and fell back on his comfy sofa.

It was only a few minutes before the phone rang. "Martin, it's Brendan. I noticed that there was something between you and Charles today – or was I imagining things?"

"What do you mean, Brendan?"

"I thought there was – perhaps not, as you seemed to get on well. Maybe I was wrong."

"Leave it, Brendan. I knew him in the past but let's leave it there."

"OK. Before I go, I thought it was worth mentioning that this Charles guy is sound; he has joined our little community and fitted in well."

"I am sure he has." Martin wondered where this was going.

"You will not know the situation, but since meeting Naomi he has formed an association with her and he is helping her to find her kids; he is a humane guy, totally committed to the cause."

"Yes, I have heard," Martin clarified.

"He spends all day sending letters all over the world, spends his own money travelling to clarify leads, and I cannot think of a better person."

"Why are you telling me this, old mate?"

There was silence for a few minutes. "'Cause I like him, and feel that he has done something in the past that you did not approve of, and you felt uncomfortable in his presence." Brendan breathed out hard.

"I have to go. I need to prepare for the trade fair; I've rented out the main outdoor stadium."

"That sounds fantastic, and I look forward to it. Thanks for listening to my woes."

"Not a problem, old mate; see you next week and we can talk then."

Martin carefully put the phone back on its hook. He needed to know how to explain the situation to his friends, and what he should do about reporting this to MI6.

Martin lived in a house on the outskirts of Kitwe, shared with a workmate called Nat Crute. Nat was a remarkable man from the north of England. He was middle-aged, quietly spoken and would do anything to help others, and his claim to fame was that he had once been a finalist in the *News of the World* darts championship.

Crute was someone who would be on your side when you most needed a friend, but he had a nervous disposition, which had developed after a mining accident. It was an unfortunate affair: he had been knocked unconscious by falling rock and trapped for many hours. When the rescue squad found him, they had a tedious job getting him to the surface. He survived, and was eventually invalided out of the mining industry only to start working in the oil and gas sector, but the ordeal had left its mark and he avoided all excitement or impending danger.

During their stay in the house he and Martin had become firm friends, but on one occasion the project manager rebuked Martin over an incident that involved both of them.

DOES A GIFT FROM A FRIEND ALWAYS BRING HAPPINESS?

Charles was receiving presents from a local man by the name of George Mwanza. In lieu of a payment of a loan Mwanza still owed Charles money and had promised to pay him back when they next met but in the meantime he continued to send a few presents in friendship.

Charles was appreciative of Mwanza's goodwill, but passed the presents on to his old friend Martin, whom he was trying to flatter.

At first it was an eight-foot python skin, rolled up and treated, which Martin hung on his wall. The next was a full leopard skin, and when Martin received this he put it on the floor of his bedroom.

The last gift he'd received caused a lot of trouble. The crocodile was over ten feet long – head, claws, eyes, tail and teeth – and delivered rolled up, and Martin had difficulty rolling the beast into the bathroom. Finally he managed to lay it in the bath – the head at one end, claws over the side and tail halfway up the wall; it nearly touched the showerhead.

When the unsuspecting Nat arrived home and went to the bathroom he did not expect to meet up with a scowling crocodile, and had quite a shock!

The incident was one of gossip among the expatriate group and the thought of Nat nearly having a heart attack was thought of as dark humour. But when the story got to the ears of the Project Director he took a dim view of it and reprimanded Martin both for his collection of dead animals and the act of nearly scaring Nat to death.

The deceased crocodile, snake and leopard were removed from the house.

24

TRUST IN AN OLD FRIEND

Charles was looking forward to seeing Naomi. He had left Nkana Golf Club a little inebriated, and drove slowly and carefully – he needed to if he was to survive the exit road. On the way home he gave a lot of thought to his meeting on the course with Martin.

When the heat had initially been put on him at Sullom Voe, he had suspected it was Martin who was the culprit who exposed him. Then later, during gym sessions, he was conscious of Valeron's actions and mannerisms and felt as though he was setting him up.

It seemed to Charles at the time that he was devising tasks for him, including visiting the IRA's operations cottage in Brae, a secret location where they could link Charles and his colleague to bomb making.

Could he trust him now? He was prepared to put things behind him and move on, but what if Martin did not feel the same way? He could set him up again. He'd seemed relaxed after the golf, but Charles would need to steer him and persuade Martin not to mention their meeting with anyone especially George Webster – he was sitting on a tightrope.

That evening it was a peaceful time for Charles and Naomi; they were excited about their recent endeavours, and hoped they would get some positive return from them. He had made contact with a friend from Zimbabwe – he had met this guy at the pub in Ndola, but later he'd lost his employment and moved back to Bulawayo. His name was Chola, and during one routine telephone conversation he'd mentioned that he knew of a Ghanaian family who lived in the neighbourhood, and promised to investigate.

They'd also heard from a lady in Nigeria, but soon the conversation dwindled; she, like many others, was trying to see how much money was in it for her.

"Please do not let your hopes run too wild in the first instance; nearly all the information we have received so far has suggested a hoax," Charles warned.

"Yes, we must be careful, and I understand fully, but I am always hoping that the next telephone call we get will be a good one," said Naomi.

"In the case of Zimbabwe I will send Chola a note asking him to verify the information about the family he mentioned.

"However, a note came to me from a family in a place called Maputo on the east coast of Africa." Charles was matter-of-fact.

"Maputo, yes, I know exactly where that is; it sounds a good possibility, the sort of place that Kwasi would go to hide with his girlfriend."

"You do not know that she is even still with him, or if the kids are with him." Charles was trying to be constructive.

"Anyway, what shall we do with this one?" asked Naomi.

"I will try to make contact." Charles got up. "Like some tea, or would you prefer a beer?"

He had requested the information he wanted from Chola, but never heard from him again.

A day before the meeting between Martin and Charles, Nat and Charles drove home for lunch. Martin was always trying to defeat Nat at darts; they had erected a board in the house, and often played during their lunch break, but Martin could never beat him.

It was a hot day, and they had finished their lunch. James, the houseboy, was clearing the table. Moving from the table and settling on the sofa, they had half an hour for a quick nap. Nat lay down and closed his eyes, and fell into a deep sleep.

With just two minutes remaining before they returned to work, Martin woke up Nat with a loud, "Time to go, Nat."

Nat jumped up quickly and made for the door, but Martin held out the darts and said, "Come on, Nat, just time for a quick game."

"Do we have enough time?"

"Of course, it will only take a few minutes."

Martin got off with a double and with Nat still trying to focus on the board; then he finished up with a double eight. He turned to Nat. "Sorry, mate, it's my game."

"Nah, best of three," Nat said. He was now wide awake.

"Sorry, Nat, no time, I have a meeting. Come on, I'll drive."

Martin was happy; he had achieved the impossible. The terms were dodgy, but all's fair in fun and war.

Just as they were leaving the phone rang.

"I'll get it, Nat, you just take some deep breaths."

"Hello, is that you, Martin? Webster here."

"Hi, George." He rolled his eyes as it was an inappropriate time, especially if he was to talk about his association with Charles. "What can I do for you?"

"It concerns our friend Coughlin," said Webster. "It seems that he actually absconded from both Sullom Voe and the IRA at the same time."

Martin welcomed this news in light of his forthcoming meeting with Charles. "Interesting," he answered.

"Yes, but that is only half the story, because he wowed a widow in London, duped her and stole her husband's personal details and his money." George was picking up the pace.

"So he is now not only an inactive terrorist, but also a fraudster and a thief?" The voice tailed off; Martin was trying to sound enthusiastic.

"One way of putting it; however, we have had some luck in tracking him." George was getting to the point.

"Where does the track take you, George – surely not here in Kitwe?"

"We know what continent he is on, and the section of the continent he is operating in, and what we have discovered is that he is heading in your direction, although possibly a few thousand miles short of you yet."

"Do you want me to keep a lookout, George? I meet lots of expats, especially in my spare-time role of promoter." Martin was leading his man.

"That's the reason for the call, old boy; ring me with anything you think will help us clear this matter up."

"Of course – remember last time?"

"Yes I do, and bloody good show; hope the same will happen this time. Anyway, do that for me and we will speak in two weeks or so – that's if you do not ring me in the meantime."

"Absolutely, George."

The line went dead.

Martin slumped back in his chair. Webster's call had presented him with a dilemma.

"Come on, bonny lad, we must fly; it's already quarter past the hour." Nat was joking; he never worried. He appreciated Martin was stressed, and said nothing about the trick his friend had played on him.

On Wednesday, Charles agreed to meet Martin in Kitwe; he paid a mineworker to take him in his car. They agreed to meet at a restaurant run by a German lady – the cuisine was European and the local cooks had an excellent reputation.

AN OVERDUE MEETING

He arrived early and a little shaken as the old car taking him from Ndola to Kitwe was unstable. The driver looked either inebriated or stoned, and he was thankful when he arrived and left the driver to sleep off whatever he was suffering from.

Charles had made himself comfortable and had already ordered a drink when Martin arrived. He was smiling, which was a good sign, and he shook Charles's hand firmly.

"Do I call you Barney or Charles? It is all rather confusing for me at the moment," said Martin, and Charles wasn't sure whether this was sarcasm or jest.

"Call me Charles, if you don't mind; it's just that everyone around here knows me by that name."

"OK, it's Charles. Now please, old mate, I would appreciate it if you can be honest with me and tell me your story – the truth, please – and we can order some food in the meantime."

"It can be only that, and my thanks for not saying anything at the golf course."

"My pleasure, Charles, but I cannot promise to keep the terms of our previous friendship under wraps forever."

"In Sullom Voe I worked on the site, but had been recruited and trained by the IRA." Charles paused, then continued. "It was my job as an agent to use an IED at the opening ceremony in May 1981, but with only six months to go I saw sense. It was a senseless thing to get involved with, and I absconded."

"What made you change your mind?"

"The senseless killings of innocent people – Lord Mountbatten, children, passers-by. It was too much, I just knew I had to get out, but when I did, I knew it would create a chasing pack."

"Has it?" Martin asked.

"I don't know but I just need to be careful; it may also depend on how you react."

"I need more time to think, Charles."

"I would appreciate some time also. I have not hurt a fly to this date, yet if I am detained, it will be either death or a long term in jail."

"Look, Charles, I am in a spot. I report to an MI6 contact, but I believe you and I also understand that you are genuinely helping others, so I may well not say anything at this moment. However, I will need to come up with a diversion, especially with Webster breathing down my neck."

"Thank you, Martin, I am in your debt."

There was a pause, and Martin wasn't sure whether he had said the right thing. He had not mentioned that he was aware that Charles had stolen from the deceased husband; a serious offence, and he would need to warn him in due course.

"Come, Martin, let me buy you dinner; it's all I can do."

"No, that's kind of you but I have a big tournament coming up and I need to talk things through with my partner, Wolfgang. We should meet again tomorrow; I will come to Ndola at about 4pm if that's all right, because there is something you must know."

25

A BLIND DATE

"Ba Naomi, what about a game of cards, so I can win some money from you?"

"Now why do you call me Ba Naomi, when you don't know what it means?" Naomi flashed a beaming smile at Brendan.

"Beautiful Naomi," mimicked Brendan, "would you like to play cards with my friends? It would be good if we can get six players, and with that many, I can win more money."

"But it's curfew, Ba Brendan; when do we play?"

"Now, my dear Naomi, so let us all sit around the table and play like good children. And by the way, you have met my good friend Charles haven't you? He has come all the way from Ireland to play cards with you."

"Yes Charles is helping me find my children, we have met a few times and Charles has carried out lots of research."

Charles glanced at Naomi sitting to his left. She seemed embarrassed by Brendan's comment. "I can see why you were good at sports." He tried to put her at ease. "That is, being tall and athletic-looking."

"I like sports, especially netball." Her heavy Afrikaans accent was prominent.

Charles had already met her at a previous party and after speaking with her then and a few times since on the telephone he had never really appreciated her poise and elegance, she appeared to him previously as a woman in need of help, nothing more. Now in her presence again, he found her a different person. Charles studied her face, trying to be inconspicuous, and gently asked her questions, utilising her answers to cleverly turn the subject of the conversation to a common interest.

Her features were typically soft and African: slightly rounded nose, deep brown eyes, a high forehead, her lips beautifully formed. The best was her smile; rarely used, it lit up the room when she did. She spoke English well, although heavily accented; she had learnt German at boarding school and spoke many African dialects. Her native language was Afrikaans.

She looked at Charles, her expression innocent. "But who told you that I was good at sports?"

"It was Brendan, I have to admit; "I'm not famous." She smiled, accepting the compliment.

Charles noticed her large, elegant hands gracefully moving around the table; sometimes as a gesture, other times when dealing the cards. Either way, they moved with poise and grace. Her dress was not elegant, it was as if she had just finished the housework, but it was tight-fitting and emphasised the shapely contours of her body.

"I must go to the bathroom." She rose slowly, pulled down her dress over her long brown legs, and walked away under Charles's gaze. He noticed that her feet, like her hands, were large but elegant. Graceful and sure-footed, with a stealthy lope, she walked like an antelope.

After Naomi disappeared from view Charles became aware of the amusement of the others, who were following his gaze.

"Come, let's play cards." Veronica placed a pack in the centre of the table.

"OK, Veronica, but the only game you girls seem to know is rummy," joked Brendan.

"Is it rummy? Oh, I hope so." Naomi returned to the table and joined the five people already seated. She sounded like an appreciative child.

Brendan and Veronica sat on one side of the table, with Jim and Pet opposite and Charles and Naomi adjacent to them; Jim suggested that with six players another pack of cards should be introduced, and he added these to those already on the table and shuffled them thoroughly.

"No cheating, beautiful Naomi," Brendan teased mischievously.

They cut for the deal.

"Oh good, it's mine – I have the queen," said Naomi. She dealt.

"Cut them first," Brendan joked.

"OK, OK." She gracefully gathered the cards in, shuffled them and dealt them, then when she was finished placed those that were left on the table.

After a number of pickups, Charles noticed that Naomi dropped her hands, exposing her cards. Her hand consisted of four sevens, two threes and a jack, and his consisted of a four, a five, a six, three queens, and a three. At the first chance he picked from the top of the pack; it was a queen. Holding back from a winning declaration should he use the queen, he instead kept it and threw down his three, deliberately forfeiting winning the game.

Naomi was quickly onto the card and shouted, "Rummy! I have won, that is marvellous." She laughed, and those at the table were surprised; it was the first spontaneous laugh they had heard from her for a long time.

Brendan got up. "I am going to bed; this game is too stressful." He grabbed Veronica's hand and they made for the bedroom, and Jim and Petula idled to the kitchen, leaving Charles and Naomi to gather up the cards.

She was so excited about her winning hand, showing unbridled emotion as she laughed and clapped with joy. She was still laughing when from the table she picked up Charles's discarded hand and carefully inspected the cards.

"That is a shame," she murmured, and rose steadily from the table. "Come, Charles, I have a bone to pick with you." And they walked to the room allocated to her. " We can share the same room can't we, Charles, I hope my offer is not too forward for you?"

Charles cleared his throat. "No. Not at all Naomi."

Naomi returned from the bathroom; she wore a white robe and, it seemed, nothing underneath. She did not look at him, but tilted her head to the ceiling and spoke. "The curtains, Charles, they are open. Are you going to stand there in that position all night?"

Charles felt like a child, he closed the curtains as instructed and moved to the bathroom where he cleaned his teeth and undressed, and after a few minutes walked coyly back into the room. Naomi was lying on her back, her hair pulled straight back, her eyes still on the ceiling. She ignored Charles for the moment.

As he got into bed, she spoke to him slowly. "Charles, I am not myself, and something happened a few weeks ago that has scared me."

"Anything to do with your family?"

"No."

"What was it?" Charles was puzzled.

"It happened on the road to Luanshya…"

26

ON THE ROAD TO LUANSHYA

Naomi related the story exactly as it had happened and made no excuse for being in the car. After a pause, she finished her explanation. "It was circumstance; nothing wrong happened but I should not have been there, and you, under the current circumstances, may be cavorting with a felon."

Charles did not want to be associated with the police in any way, nor did he want to block his friendship that he had with Naomi so he stalled the conversation to think of a solution.

"I did telephone Pet for help and told her what happened; she is trying to find out the details, but in the meantime, I understand he is alive. I may or may not get involved, but thought it best to explain the situation."

She turned over on her side and Charles heard her sobbing. He looked down at her long brown back; she looked vivacious, hair spilling over her shoulders onto the pillow. On the bedside table he noticed a thin string of beads; a leather tab was attached, and on closer inspection he read a number – probably meaningless, except that the beads were smeared with blood.

"Naomi, this situation appears to be becoming more dangerous by the minute, and by getting involved you may now be linked to something you do not understand."

"What do you mean, Charles?"

"Khakkeki may be working for a cartel, a mob or any type of organised crime gang that would wipe you out in a second if they thought you knew something about them."

"What do you want me to do about it?"

"Naomi, this is serious. It would be better if you moved away from Kitwe for a few weeks until this situation blows over."

"Move away? Where would I go?"

"Do you think that others knew you were in the room waiting for him?" Charles was trying to establish her level of involvement.

Naomi shook her head, her eyes wide open but seeing nothing.

Charles continued to stare at the beads. "Did you leave any identification in the room?"

She did not answer, but after a few moments she turned over and looked directly at him. "I should not have told you, Charles. It was wrong of me, and does not involve you – please forget what I said, and we'll split in the morning."

"That is too late, Naomi; let us overcome this together." He did not believe what he was saying; he was thinking of his own survival. "We will talk in the morning and make a plan." Unfortunately, he was now in this situation up to his neck.

She turned away from him again and her sobs grew soft, they subsided shortly after as she fell asleep.

Charles had lost his tiredness; his mind was racing. Why had he got involved in something that might bring him unwanted exposure? Who had attacked James Khakkeki, and why? Africa was a dark place; life was cheap and killings occurred every night. He did not want to become part of those statistics.

He then fell into a deep sleep, a nightmare brewing in his mind.

It took him into a dark period of violence and death; it was early evening, and directly in front of him a huge man held a steel axe, more like an Indian tomahawk. He was felling a tree, and glanced at Charles. "You to be next."

A group of women stood over a fire close by, and one of them was much darker and taller than the rest. It was Naomi, and watching her not thirty yards away was a group of African men. They looked dishevelled, unkempt and very threatening.

Milling around behind the women was another group, of mixed gender. They were wailing and screaming as if to scare away the men who were watching with intent. They held rocks in one hand and long knives in the other, and they just stared at those around the fire.

Then one of the men at the back shouted, "Give to us the secret number or we will kill you all and feed you to the buzzards."

The women wailed even louder, and the men shouted appeals to those who were threatening. The armed men started to charge, their long knives at the ready—

"Charles, Charles, wake up!"

Charles jumped up and out of bed, crying out, yet still asleep.

"Steady on, old man." It was Brendan.

"What's up? Who are those men?" Charles was sweating profusely. "Get away!" he shouted. Then he woke, and noticed it was Brendan before him, and he held no knife.

"I must have been having a terrible dream." Charles stared at his friend, white-faced and naked.

Brendan laughed. "We must go, Charles, old man, otherwise we will miss our tee-off time, knives or no bloody knives."

Glancing at the other side of the bed, Charles remembered that Naomi was resting and he noticed she was awake.

"Naomi, stay in the house, do not contact anyone about Khakkeki and we will sort this out later."

"Yes, Charles, just go and enjoy your golf."

27

A GERMAN IS IN TOWN, AUGUST 1980

Wolfgang Schmidt decided to take a long weekend. He usually worked six and a half days a week, but a few days away from his engineering company would give him some rest. He had persevered for nearly twenty years but now it was time he took a holiday.

A huge man, tall with wide shoulders, Wolfgang did not suffer fools gladly. He was renowned for speaking his mind, and there were not many men who would oppose him. His bark and his bite were too much of a challenge.

His main clients were the Copperbelt mining companies, and his Germanic gift for producing quality precision items provided a generous amount of work and earned him a good standard of living.

Although German by birth he rarely travelled back to his home country, preferring instead to stay close to his adopted country and enjoy what it had to offer. With few luxuries available in Zambia there were adequate other pastimes on offer, including fishing on the Zambezi and hunting in the Luangwa Valley; he had a permit from the government to 'cull' five game animals a year.

He was a natural businessman and floated his company on the financial markets, selling at a high price and buying back his own shares when the price was low.

Also an ambitious man, he had originally migrated to Johannesburg after finishing his engineering apprenticeship, then found work and accommodation in the area. It was a rough neighbourhood and it wasn't long before he encountered the wrong type of people; on one occasion he got involved in a fight and knocked two of the attackers unconscious.

Two nights later the men, accompanied by two others, attacked the German from behind and stabbed him many times, piercing his lung. Wolfgang crawled to the local hospital, nearly a mile away from where he was attacked; he survived and spent the next few weeks recovering there.

Six weeks later he paid a taxi driver to drive him to a bar where his perpetrators were drinking and asked the driver to lure them outside. The taxi driver parked close to the bar and waited until the gang appeared at the door. Wolfgang then produced his hidden shotgun and opened both barrels; two of the men fell to the ground and the third retreated back into the bar.

The shocked driver reluctantly took his orders from Wolfgang and made off at speed to Jan Smuts Airport, where the German boarded a flight to Victoria Falls. The driver returned slowly to his base in Johannesburg where he knew the police would question him. He did expect to be interrogated, and Wolfgang had given him five hundred rand in case he needed to pay his way out of trouble.

Wolfgang had planned the getaway with German precision; both the flight time and his intended two-day stay at Victoria Falls. He knew that if he could find out who the most corrupt customs officers were, he could negotiate some 'financial agreement' that would allow him to slip across the border into Zambia without too much ado.

Arriving at Victoria Falls Airport, he opted in the first instance to check in to Peters Place, a small hotel on the outskirts of town. It was a roadhouse, not particularly attractive but built in a good strategic position on top of the hill; an excellent surveillance spot from where he could monitor vehicles more easily. He paid in advance and kept out of the way of other guests, especially tourists; he ate all of his meals in his room; and on the second day made his first move and booked a taxi to the airport. It would give him a chance to evaluate the situation before making his move.

The border control between Zimbabwe and Zambia consists of a twin path, one for entry and the other for departure and the paths edged with high vertical aluminium security posts. When a change of staff is required, or in an emergency, a locked gate is accessible for use by the officers only, and this would allow them to bypass the queue.

Wolfgang was stood assessing the situation when he became aware of an argument that was taking place at the entry side of the path. It was soon to become very noisy, with both sides showing aggression.

Then, after further bluster and swagger, it became violent, with punches exchanged. The officers on duty were distracted and moved to separate the warring groups; this gave Wolfgang an opportunity and, checking that he carried his passport, he glided quietly through the unlocked access gate and slipped into Zambia with nothing more than the clothes he wore.

Now in another country, he was faced with his biggest challenge. Little money, no contacts, no vehicle – he needed a plan if he was to survive.

He found work in the trucking industry and started driving long-haul shuttles between the Copperbelt and Dar es Salaam in Tanzania. It was good money, and during his driving years he banked every penny he earned. His savings working excessive overtime were to help him set up an engineering company, and over the following years he slowly built up a financially successful company. He married a Zimbabwean lady and had three daughters, lived a very rich life in a poor country, and his best holidays were enjoyed on Zambian soil, either in the Luangwa Valley or fishing on the Zambezi.

But his new life was beginning in the boxing world.

28

A BOXING BONANZA

In the spring of 1980 Wolfgang was interested to read in the *Times* that a new boxing promoter had arrived in Kitwe and was becoming popular with the local talent.

He was especially impressed that the top Zambian world and Olympic boxers would be turning professional and training at the Rokana gym; it would be the first professional promotion in Kitwe for twenty years. The first show would be a dinner and boxing event staged at the Hotel Edinburgh.

Later that day Wolfgang made a point of purchasing two tables at the ringside; his sixteen tickets were spread among his favourite clients.

During the run-up to the show, Martin's mother died and it was necessary for him to fly back to the UK to attend her funeral. It was a sad time for him, and all he wanted was to be left alone, but it was not to be!

Returning from the UK, he was waiting to board a flight at Heathrow when he got into a conversation with an Irishman who turned out to be a professional snooker player. His name was Jackie Ray and he was sponsored (paid to perform snooker tricks) at the snooker club in Kitwe.

It was early morning, and with a lot of drink inside him, Ray could not stop talking. It was difficult for Martin to escape from the Irishman, and when he did, he made sure that he kept away from him for the rest of the journey. Occasionally during the flight Martin would look down the plane and see, above the heads of the other passengers, whom Jackie was still talking to, drinking and keeping everyone in his vicinity awake. Martin thought what a relief it was not to be near him; there would be no peace.

Martin changed planes at Lusaka and boarded the flight to Kitwe. He was careful to select a seat in the free seating zone at the back of the plane, where he thought he could hide away from Jackie or anyone else who might disturb him.

A few minutes after boarding, he had made himself comfortable in his seat when he felt a hand on his shoulder. "Is that where you are, my boy? So now we can catch up and I can enjoy the next hour in your company."

The hour's flight to Kitwe was more than comfortable; so much so that Martin could hardly walk on leaving the plane, he was so intoxicated. He had broken his rule of never drinking before twelve o'clock midday, but it was done; the smooth talking Irishman succeeded but at the end of the day this encounter brought dividends for Martin; as Jackie had bought three tables (or twenty-four seats) for his boxing show!

Commercially the preparations for the show were proceeding well; tickets were almost sold out two weeks before the date.

Wolfgang was so impressed with the set-up, it seemed he was spending more time with the promotion than he was with his own engineering business.

On the day of the show Martin decided to play in a golf competition at Nkana; probably an unwise thing to do in light of the responsibility that the show was on that evening but he thought everything was organised sufficiently to do so.

All tickets sold and all preparations in hand. He would play in the morning and finish around one o'clock; that would give him five hours to dress and welcome the guests.

The golf was painfully slow and did not finish until 4.30, and Martin did not actually arrive at the hotel until 6.30. By a stroke of luck Charles had pulled out of the golf the previous day and promised Martin that he would call down to the venue and make sure everything was going to plan. He arrived at two in the afternoon and was still there organising when Martin arrived. Charles's intervention was invaluable and saved the day; had it not been for him, the event could have proved embarrassing for his friend.

"Have you been busy?" Martin asked his friend.

"Nothing much, Martin; just unlocked the dressing rooms, made sure the kitchen is staffed and that all the barmen are prepared and ready to go." Casually, he added, "Then I met the television producer and together we set up cameras, then ensured that the ticket office is open and all's well! Don't worry, it was the least I could do for an old friend." He rolled his eyes, smiling as he did so.

Martin was so relieved to see that all the seats were full of what seemed to be happy people, and the buzz from them filled him with satisfaction. He was in Charles debt, and that was not a bad day's work for an former IRA agent.

The show turned out to be an amazing success. The press reported that it was an astonishing promotion, and brought the good old times back to Kitwe.

However, one embarrassing problem came to light after the show when the main sponsor claimed that one letter had been missing from their company name which had been painted on the ring-post covers. Nobody seemed to notice at the time, and Martin looked into the reason why this had occurred.

It became apparent that when the painting contractor carried out the work, he ran out of space and deleted one letter, but did not inform the promoter of this, and it nearly cost Martin dearly. The error could have been expensive as the sponsor threatened litigation, but the situation was settled amicably when Martin promised to give them the same service for free at the next promotion.

When the balance of accounts was produced the profit margins were minimal but at least not in the red; it was a good return considering it was the first show of its kind in Kitwe for two decades.

DIFFERENCE IN CLASS

The corporate details for the Boxing company were soon set up, with Martin and Wolfgang as directors and Lemmie as matchmaker, but it wasn't long before a misunderstanding occurred between the German and the old boxer.

Lemmie represented a prominent engineering supplier, and this clashed with Wolfgang's role as CEO of an engineering company, for it could be seen as complicity if the two did business together. It was discussed between the parties involved and it seemed that Lemmie was to be the loser. He resigned from his role in the boxing world where he had once been the hero.

Over the next couple of months this situation weighed on Martin's conscience, as he felt a loyalty to Chipili, who had been his main support in difficult times and now he had deserted him.

Lemmie was a living legend in the world of Zambian boxing. An infamous Zambian sportsman helping to dismantle white supremacy after independence, he was the catalyst that provided confidence to young black Africans, giving them the will to win out in the face of adversity.

The Zambian government recognised his achievements and efforts in the struggle for independence. They subsequently offered him the position of Zambian High Commissioner to the Congo, and he held office in Lubumbashi for some years after the dissolution of his partnership with Martin and Wolfgang. He died after suffering a heart attack whilst still in office.

29

A STAR IS BORN,
NOVEMBER 1980

The boxing shows in Kitwe were always popular, especially when well-known international fighters competed. However, one man who was not known to the public in the early days later became a legend – his name was Benson Chisala.

Benson was a miner, not tall but with a fantastic body, and was known around the mines for his muscles, his smile and his wave. No one was sure exactly how old he was, and until boxing came to Kitwe he had never had an organised fight in his life.

At first glance Benson looked menacing; his face cut as if by stone, his broad shoulders and angular shape, his eyes hard and piercing, although in a second he would give a friendly greeting and a wave; he embraced life with happiness.

When the gym first opened and the professionals were in regular training, Benson was always at the back of the hall, watching and waiting. After a while he came forward and persuaded Martin to allow him to work out with the established fighters.

Most of the boxers in training laughed when Benson joined them. After all, he was keen, not young and, according to them, not particularly talented.

He worked out relentlessly and trained like a gladiator; even when he donned the gloves for sparring, his demeanour changed. He became focused and driven, moving as smooth as silk as naturally as if he were a born athlete and the first to understand when and how to move around the ring. Although he was a novice at the gym he had natural ability and soon became a sparring partner for the more astute fighters.

He fought a draw on his first bout. He was never in trouble, although throughout the fight he continually looked in Martin's direction, as if to seek approval. His second fight he won on points, mainly by moving around his opponent and using his jab, and again always looking outside the ring for judgement.

He progressed steadily, and after three fights, his record stood at two wins and a draw. Martin was approached by the Zimbabwean promoter Dave Wellings, who proposed a match between his boxer Smart Thompson and Chisala. Both were welterweights, although Thompson was renowned for his punching prowess and had vastly more experience than Benson; he had a remarkable record, with sixty per cent of his wins coming by way of a knockout.

Martin and Wolfgang were both sceptical about taking on the fight, especially given their boxer's inexperience, and decided to discuss the matter further with Benson. But his answer was, "If you want me to fight this man, boss, then I will fight him." This attitude was not what they were looking for!

Martin finally relented, and Benson was included on the undercard of Francis Musankabala's title fight. That night the hall was packed to the rafters, and it did not help matters when the fans without tickets accessed the show by way of an open window. Martin was under the impression that a person from the inside opened the window and it was big enough to fit a donkey in. The major problem was the maximum persons allowed under the stadium's fire regulations was exceeded by 20 per cent and cancelling was not an option; the crowd were up for it and it would have caused a riot should this particular show be called off.

Although on the undercard Benson's fight with Thompson was scheduled to take place just ahead of the main event, he was extremely nervous before the bout, and his jaw muscles twitched constantly as he was introduced. His popularity was unbelievable and this was proven by the reception he received; the sound was positively deafening.

The hall fell silent for the first round, and remained that way until near the end of the round, when a huge groan from the crowd filled the hall. Benson was felled and appeared to be unconscious lying on the canvas, just as the bell sounded.

Martin approached him quickly. He tried to sit him up, but Benson just lolled back onto the ring floor, blood coming from his nose and a cut just under his eyebrow. His eyes, bloodshot and unresponsive, did not seem to be focusing. Martin slapped him; the din had now risen from a hush at knock-down to a crescendo, but the seconds were ticking away.

Martin shouted above the noise, "Benson, get a grip – these guys are shouting for you. Stand up and grip my shoulders, then we will squat together. Come on – one, two…"

They both did three squats. Martin slapped him again and guided him back to his corner, and Benson slumped on the stool.

"How long?" Martin shouted.

"Twenty-five seconds left," Wolfgang replied.

"Ice on his neck." Martin then turned to his support below the ring. "Fill me a bucket of water."

The trainer poured every drop of water he had into the bucket and passed it to Martin. "Five seconds remaining," he shouted.

Martin threw the bucket of water directly into Benson's face. It flooded the floor, and some spilt over Wolfgang, but most of it went over the boxer, who gasped for air.

The referee quickly came over. "We cannot start the third round with this water everywhere; clear it up, and be quick."

Everyone involved with the mopping operation worked in slow motion, and forty-five seconds had elapsed before the referee called both boxers to the centre of the ring.

Martin held Benson back. "One chance, old mate."

Benson's eyes were wide and his glare menacing as he moved to the centre of the ring. Before Martin had reached the bottom of the steps, a deafening roar stopped him in his tracks; over six hundred pairs of feet stamping on the wooden terraces of the old mine hall.

Martin looked up and saw Thompson flat on the canvas. The boxer tried to raise his head; it moved only inches from the canvas. The count reached ten and after the count finished the noise continued as Thompson was attended by his trainers.

Although exhausted himself, Martin scrambled up the steps to congratulate Benson but when he reached the boxer he noticed that he was spaced out; his eyes were not focusing.

Wolfgang in the meantime was excited. "I cannot believe it – how did he find the strength?" A large grin spread across his typically placid face.

Benson was also still out on his feet, veins bulging all over his body. Blood and sweat were wiped from his face, and Martin sat him on the stool, put ice on his face and instructed him to breathe deeply and slowly. It was only after nearly five minutes that he left for the dressing room – the noise from the crowd was ear-splitting!

His popularity at the mine rocketed; he was a hero. People spoke about him, and the news spread around the Copperbelt. The newspapers gave him sporting headlines, and it seemed that all he wanted in life was to be recognised for what he was.

Chisala did have one more fight when he challenged for the Zambian welterweight title. It was his fifth professional bout and he went all of fifteen rounds only to lose to the holder, and when the gong sounded at the end he returned to his corner. Although his eyes were twinkling, he looked exhausted.

"Unlucky, mate; you gave it your all." Martin patted him on the shoulder.

"No, boss, I am the lucky one – thank you!"

When Benson visited Martin in his mine office two weeks later his purse money was in an envelope on the desk.

"No, master; the money is meaningless, I do not need it; there are others that are in need of it more than me." There was a pause, then he went on. "I have received so much adulation and good cheer from my fellow miners; it is more than I have ever expected or deserved. I have been privileged to have had such a wonderful but short career, and for this I am grateful to you." He picked up the envelope. "I will take this money, but it is not for me; it is for others, you will understand of my decision to retire."

There was a sequel to the Benson story that prevented a serious situation for Martin. He was invited to present prizes at an amateur youth event that was held in the township; a dangerous place for a white man to go alone.

As Martin walked into the hall where the fight was to be held he was violently jostled by two youths who were obviously looking for trouble.

Just before the tournament was due to start, the familiar but unexpected smiling face of Benson appeared. They hugged and shook hands.

"Enjoy, boss, and if you want anything, I am here," the ex-boxer advised.

"Thanks, Benson, but I am sure I will be OK."

At the interval Martin was again breached, and one of the men whispered, "Wrong time, wrong place – we will be waiting."

At the end of the show when he walked to his car the two guys tailed him, and Martin feared for his life.

No sooner had he opened the door and sat on his seat than the door was snatched from his hand and they were pulling him out. But as quickly as it had started, it seemed to finish, and he fell back onto his seat, gasping for air.

He tried to stabilise himself. There was lots of shouting and a crunching sound from beside his car, then silence. Martin was confused, and he was about to start the car for a quick getaway when a familiar face appeared at the window.

"You OK, master? Those guys are bad but they will not trouble you again." Benson tapped on the roof. "Safe journey, boss."

Martin carefully drove past the two inert bodies on the ground and accelerated towards Kitwe. He never saw Benson again.

During his two years of promoting and training professional boxers in Africa, Martin provided the springboard for two of his fighters to reach the top. It was to be their pinnacle. He had given them a chance for stardom, to provide them with a better life – and to further his own goal of producing a world champion. They had returned the compliment by winning virtually all of their fights and were first-class ambassadors for Zambia.

However, the priorities for the stable were clear, a step in the big time. The first opportunity came when his light middleweight John Mwamba was contracted to fight against John Mugabi in front of forty thousand loyal supporters in Lusaka.

It was an eliminator that would propel the winner into the World Top Ten, but the fight turned out to be a disaster for Martin as Mwamba lost in front of his home crowd.

30

AN OFFER THAT CANNOT BE REFUSED

Charles had found life interesting during his stay in Ndola. He felt completely at ease with life, he was enjoying his golf, and had made friends with a beautiful African girl.

He now had purpose, perhaps a cause: to help with something that would make someone else happy. He could add tenacity to enthusiasm and provide funds or anything else that would help his friend to find her children.

Charles continued to rent his house from a dodgy mineworker. He was aware the deal might fall through at any time, so kept his options open, and continued his life as normal. He rounded off his domestic life by hiring a house guard and a gardener; he paid them on a weekly basis. He did not travel outside of Ndola very much, but regularly kept in touch with his friends from Kitwe and promised to play golf with them at least on a monthly basis.

During one of these games, Brendan asked Charles if he would like to join them for a charity golf day that was to be held at the Nkana course in Kitwe.

"It will be great fun, and you can partner me on a 'better ball' basis with your old friend Martin." ('Better ball' being a competition in golf where if two play two then the best score of each two wins.)

"That sounds fine, I will be there," enthused Charles.

He was looking forward to the game, and with three weeks to go he started practising with intent. One afternoon, after returning home from a practice session, he answered a knock on the door. It was his hired guard, Joseph.

"Bwana, there is man who wants to speak with you. He is at the gate, I do not know his name but he lives just over the road." Joseph paused. "Bwana, please be aware that this man is dangerous, so please be careful."

"Why is he dangerous?" asked Charles.

"People say that he is a hawk who only works at night; his many trucks you will hear going past your house all night long, and they go into the yard behind his place. His house is only fifty metres from here." And Joseph pointed in the direction of the man's house.

"Anything else, Joseph?" enquired Charles.

"I have heard of people going into his house but never seen again."

"OK, OK, Joseph, enough of that. I promise I will be careful."

He made his way to the gate and wondered what this villain Joseph had described actually looked like.

Charles walked straight to the parked vehicle, and introduced himself as he assessed the man leaning against his bonnet. He was African, extremely dark in colour, with a broad brow and eyes that did not hold eye contact for more than the briefest of seconds.

"Hi man, my name is Godfrey Ngosa." His face changed quickly, a huge smile taking over it; his teeth were capped with gold.

They shook hands and Charles invited him into the house.

"I understand you are from England, my friend."

Charles hesitated; he did not know where this was going to lead.

Ngosa noted this and cushioned the situation. "Look, Charles, I do not want to pry into your business but I have a proposal for you." He looked for a response.

"OK, what is it?"

"I have three hundred dollars, and my sister ninety-five. I want to put it into a bank account in England, and as I know that you will visit there in the near future, I would ask that you do this favour for me. It is a cash transaction."

There was silence before Charles responded. "I have no intention of returning to the UK during the next year."

"But I can make it worthwhile if you do," added Godfrey.

They looked each other in the eye.

"I can allow you fifteen per cent of the total transaction if you can do this for me."

"But I can do the deal for you here in Zambia by going to the bank," replied Charles. Then, "Did you say three hundred and a further ninety-five dollars American?"

"But, my friend, think big: this is three hundred thousand and ninety-five thousand dollars, x1000 of which you will get nearly forty thousand dollars. You will be rich." He glared at Charles and confronted him aggressively. "Look, this is my personal account number; all you need to do is enter this number, with the bank sort code in London, and bank this for me. It will be good for both of us."

"Let me think about it. I could make a trip in a month or so."

"Very good, then let me know. I will call back in a month." He left the door open and walked out into the sunshine.

Charles waited outside the house until the bakkie reversed and drove away in a cloud of dust. He unfurled the paper the man had given him and looked at the account number; it looked familiar but he could not place its significance. He dismissed from his mind a thought that it had a strong resemblance to the one on the tag Naomi had been given by Khakkeki. He thought it a good time to clear his mind; he was excited and, with a chance of forty thousand dollars in his bank, very tempted.

He drove to the driving range; he needed the exercise.

31

DOING A GOOD DEED, NOVEMBER 1981

Later that evening, Charles sat down at his desk at home and prepared a letter that would be sent to all the major university campuses in Africa.

It read:

> *To whom it may concern*
> *From: Naomi Nzema*
> *Date: 13th November 1981*

Dear sir or madam,
Subject: missing children

The reason for this letter is to ask for your help in locating a family of three children who went missing four years ago.

The children were taken from their mother, and could now be living on the campus close to you.

If you see or hear of these children, please notify the above. They go by the names of Lisa, Clemmie and Tozer.

Sincerely,
Naomi Nzema

The destination for each letter was changed to identify the university it was intended for.

He finished late in the evening. The air was still hot, and he sat down to enjoy a cold beer, but then decided to continue his work on location hunting.

He was reviewing the various places where Naomi's children might be and was shuffling the many reports; he had his hands full when the telephone rang.

No peace for the wicked, he thought.

It was Brendan. "You still up? Not in bed?" the chirpy Irishman joked.

"Yes, of course, but I have been busy," answered Charles, not saying why.

"Thought I would tell you that I heard that six months ago a bomb exploded when the Queen was giving a speech at the place you worked in Shetland."

"Where did you hear that?" asked Charles.

"I read it in an old newspaper last week. You know what it's like here in Africa – everything is late, even important stuff like that."

"What happened, anyway?" queried Charles.

"Oh, the bomb exploded some way from the VIPs."

"Was the Queen aware of it?" Charles asked.

"Apparently she hardly moved a muscle."

"That's great; was anyone else hurt or injured?" asked Charles.

"No, but it was a different matter in Rome – the Pope was shot four times, but survived," advised Brendan.

"The Pope?!" Charles was aghast. "When?"

"The same day, I think, but I could be mistaken."

There was silence between them, each not knowing what to say.

"OK, that is unbelievable."

"Thought that I would tell you, and now I must inform Martin as I am sure he will be interested."

"I am sure he will, anyway we will catch up later in the week. We will see you later in the week."

"Look forward to it."

The line went dead.

Charles gulped his beer, deep in thought. He wondered if the two incidents were related but, feeling incredibly drowsy, he fell asleep in his chair.

His mind was in turmoil and he hardly slept; it was almost certain that Michael O'Byrne would have known something about it. His first thought was for Naomi – she needed her kids – but again if he dropped his guard it could mean curtains for him, and there would be nobody to help her.

The news concerning Pope John Paul II affected Charles. He had known nothing about it; the Pope could have been assassinated on the same day as the Queen of England. It was too painful to think about, and he could not believe that he had once been a part of it.

The attack would certainly reignite police interest and increase the pressure on him from MI6. Police would be activated around the globe and his life could be threatened. He would need to explain this to Naomi.

Another needle in the haystack was the situation in Luanshya between Naomi and Khakkeki, although now it seemed certain that Ngosa was the culprit and needed to be curtailed.

There was no alternative but to stay at home. Golf would need to be cancelled; he would think of an excuse later.

Charles thought *If the mob, alleged to be controlled by Ngosa, found out that Naomi was associated with Khakkeki they may track her to our house and kill us both.*

Next morning he was awake early, and as the sun rose above the arid bush he went for a run to clear his mind. Many Africans were already out walking to work.

32

WEEKEND MISHAP

Martin Valeron had a very busy week. He had received notification that his London-based manager on the cobalt plant was due to arrive in Zambia in a week's time to chair a meeting with the board of shareholders, and he wanted Martin to make the presentation.

The shareholders required the following:

a. Progress to date against the plan.
b. Estimated completion date.
c. Current cost against plan.
d. Final estimated cost against forecast completion.

Unfortunately for Martin, he had an international boxing tournament in Harare at virtually the same time. The flights and hotel were booked and the boxers' contracts had been signed, and now this bloody presentation.

Martin telephoned Vince Burke in his office based in Ashford, Kent.

"Hi, Vince, how are you?"

"I am fine, and looking forward to our visit next week." Vince seemed as jovial as usual.

"Is your visit definitely scheduled for next week? I have a holiday booked for that particular weekend. Can I leave Peter, my deputy, to present our position to the partners?"

"Absolutely not, out of the question!" Vince was firm. "This is the most important assembly of our financiers that we will have over the next two years, so whatever you have on, just cancel and make sure you are ready."

Martin stalled. "Have you an agenda and a script?" he asked in a moderate tone.

"Bloody right I have; I will send it to you on Wednesday, so please prepare and give me a return on Friday morning."

"OK, Vince." Martin was disappointed.

"No holiday, and I will wait for your presentation with slides on Wednesday."

The call ended.

Blast and damn, thought Martin. *I may need to cancel my trip, but this is the most important fight of the year and will determine the future. How can I get Wolfgang to understand?*

It was Friday, and too late to call on Wolfgang tonight. He decided to wait until Saturday morning and break the news to him then.

The three fights lined up for the National Stadium in Harare included his three boxing stars. It was important that he travelled with them, but then it was more important he attended the business meeting!

The more he thought about it, the more he knew he needed to be there at the ringside. The outcome of the fights would show his achievements during the last two years.

He pulled up outside Wolfgang's house, not looking forward to the forthcoming discussion.

The German's huge frame sauntered to his gate to meet his partner. "I did not expect you, but good to see you." He smiled and opened the gate that was always kept locked for security.

"Wolfgang, I have instructions to make a presentation for my company at a corporate meeting on Monday week, but as you know, our return from Harare is on Tuesday."

"You must be in Salisbury." Wolfgang seemed to ignore that the city was now called Harare.

"Wolfgang, it is more than my job is worth, but if I can work it I could be back on Sunday evening."

"That's OK with me, but the guys will be disappointed as the extra days are a bit of a holiday for them."

"OK, it is what it is; I will change my flight to arrive back on Sunday evening, and you and the boys can stay."

Martin shook hands with his partner and drove back to his house on the outskirts of Kitwe.

Back home, Martin pondered and replayed the story that Brendan had told him regarding the Sullom Voe assassination attempt. This troubled him. He needed reliable information, and the best man to update him sat at his desk in London.

He picked up the phone and dialled, his hands shaking as he did so. "George, it's me, Valeron. You remember our connection with Sullom Voe? It seems a long time ago, but I was hoping you could give me an update on the attack; as you know, we are a bit backward here in Africa."

"Hi, Martin, good to hear from you, and a few things to get you up to speed with. The first is that we have not located Coughlin yet, and we may not pursue him under the current situation; things have changed and we have bigger fish to catch. He was not involved in the final act in Shetland so we have taken the heat off him, but if you do hear anything then please do not hesitate to contact me. We always need people like you to give us a heads-up."

George thought for a moment, then must have remembered where Martin was working.

"What town are you in, old boy."

"Somewhere that nothing happens, I guess?" answered Martin.

"I remember it's Zambia but which town? he asked.

"I am in Kitwe, George, on the Copperbelt."

"Sounds interesting, but whilst we're talking about the opening ceremony, yes, one bomb did explode but it turned out to be harmless; it was detonated in the ducting inside the power station. The other, well, it was delivered late and returned from the Shetland post office to an address in the north of England."

"What was the outcome of the one that did detonate?"

"It went off, but in the structure and nobody was hurt. It was lucky but it seemed that it was dumped at the last minute, thank God."

"Anyone charged?"

"One guy caught, but we understand there were two. Anyway, the situation has not changed with Ireland; still the same difference."

There was a pause, and Martin interjected, "I will not keep you any longer, George; I am sure that you are busy with other things."

"That's all right, my friend, but keep in touch; you never know when you might find other people who may interest me."

"Bye, George."

"See you."

The phone call was terminated, but it gave Martin a lot of food for thought. Charles had got away from the site six months before the attack. He had absconded without carrying out a single act of terror and now he was a changed man, assisting those who needed it – much of his time was spent helping Naomi find her lost family. Martin now felt more comfortable with his friend, and intended to make a more serious attempt at making his feelings clear the next time they met.

He was smiling to himself, due to the relief of finding out the truth about Charles, when he was disturbed by a noise. It came from movement outside the house, and broke the stillness.

He switched out the light, and looked through the curtains. A shadow glided across the dry earth. He soon realised it was the house guard walking around the garden, trying to make his presence felt. Martin wondered what Joseph would do in the event of violent invasion; any sensible man would run and look after himself! He was nonetheless a brave man earning but a few dollars; on the other hand, he could earn more, for example as an informer against the people living in the house, if anyone was willing to pay for his services.

The slow tread of Joseph's boots on the garden outside soon faded away and the room was again quiet, with the exception of the silence of the bush outside.

"Damn it – Martin picked up the phone and rang his old buddy. "Brendan, is that you?"

"Yes, mate, it is, what can I do for you?"

"Fancy a Mosi?" (Mosi-oa-tunya is a beer named after Victoria Falls.)

"Yes, mate, normally, but not now – I am with Veronica."

"OK, sorry."

"No, don't be, but why not join us tomorrow for golf? We are playing at Mufulira."

"OK, that sounds fine."

"Yes, we are three at the moment."

"Three?"

"Yes: you, me, and a guy from the London office will join us, he's called Colin Schubert, and Charles will make it four."

"Thanks, Brendan; I'll meet you at the golf club at Muf and we can form a better ball."

"See you there. Cheers."

Martin now felt upbeat and was looking forward to the game tomorrow. He forgot the impending dangers that he dreamt regarding 'death after a break-in' and decided to go to bed; golf would take his mind off his trip next week, not to mention his meeting with the partners on Monday.

33

IN A TANGLE

Charles Siddons, alias Barney Coughlin, had travelled nearly the length of Africa to get to his current home in Ndola. How he had achieved this without a problem was a mystery to him, but it was now in the distant past.

He enjoyed the house where he lived, although he continued to suspect that the man he was renting from was on a fiddle with the mines; possibly some fraudulent deal with the mine housing association. But this was OK with Charles; it was a fair price and a perfect hideaway.

He had adequate cash to see him through the year, and could if necessary utilise money in Sarah's deceased husband's bank account; it was easy with his card but this benefit was due to end. He had done this a number of times before, and it was never ideal in Zambia to carry large amounts of cash.

At midday on Sunday, he had just finished making a curry from a few vegetables he had found at the supermarket, and put it in the freezer until he was hungry.

He heard a car pull up sharply outside, and simultaneously the phone rang. He took the phone first.

"Hi, Charley, I'm coming over, is that OK?" Naomi seemed upbeat given that she was worried about a few things.

"Of course, Naomi; get a taxi and I will settle when he arrives. Must go for now, I have another visitor outside the gate."

"OK, see you in about twenty." Naomi hung up.

Godfrey Ngosa jumped out of his car and contemptuously pushed the guard away when he saw Charles. "We do the deal I suggested last time we met, but now I want cash urgently. Now you will make double as I cut my rate."

Charles thought he was talking in riddles. "Hold up, Godfrey, what are you talking about? Just calm down." He felt perturbed at Ngosa's attitude; the man was rude and the heat did not help Charles's own mood. He started to sweat. "Godfrey, it is too hot; let's resume this conversation inside." Charles walked towards the house, but was wary of this man and was already thinking of ways to deter further conversation.

He changed his direction and moved under the banana tree, and waited for Ngosa to join him. "Now, what's on your mind, Godfrey?"

"Look, Charles, the last time we spoke I offered you a deal to make some money by putting cash through my account in London."

"Yes, I remember that, Godfrey, but at the moment I have no plans to travel." Charles was puzzled by Ngosa's urgency, but continued with some caution.

"I need some cash urgently, to travel to Senegal tomorrow. I have a bereavement, my mother has passed and funerals are expensive, so if you can forward me fifty thousand American dollars now, and once you have exchanged my money keep a further fifty for yourself, and return the rest to me."

"Godfrey, look, I do not intend to travel to London in the near future, nor do I have the money available to give to you now!"

"Mr Charles, you promised to do this deal, and now I expect you to honour your promise." He seemed desperate.

"Godfrey, with all due respect I did not promise you anything, I said I would think about it."

There was an uneasy pause in the discussion, and Godfrey took up the conversation. "You people think that you can manipulate me. I have already lost a hundred thousand dollars from a man who promised to exchange. He was African, nothing less than expected, but from you, from the UK, I expect honesty!"

"What was the man's name?" asked Charles.

"Oh, that is not important – I think it was Khakkeki, or something foreign." Godfrey's face was twitching and his eyes glazed. He turned quickly, and stormed from the garden. Charles heard the car door slam, and the engine roared as it screeched away in a cloud of dust.

Charles returned to the house and sat waiting for Naomi to arrive. He wanted to discuss with her his ideas regarding the possible location of her ex-husband Kwasi and their children, and if anything that was of use came up he would send a contact letter to the campus where Kwasi worked.

But a more pressing issue that he needed to discuss was this thing with Ngosa; his money-laundering tactics and especially his connection with Khakkeki would be interesting to Naomi. He could not wait for her to arrive so he could tell her the story.

He stayed outside and waited, but it wasn't Naomi's taxi that arrived next; it was the police. Two officers, dressed in crisp khaki denims with black peaked caps and looking extremely serious, got out of the car and approached Charles as he sauntered outside of his front door.

Charles felt that both uniforms, although recently laundered, were not the right size for these gentlemen. The wide brown belts were pulled tightly around their thick waists, each with their stomach overhanging the buckle, their rotund bottom protruding from the rear, and the hem of their jacket bent upwards due to the tightness of the belt.

"My name is Officer Makobi and this is Officer Manda; we are here to question you regarding your association with Naomi Nzema." He was very formal and sombre.

"Yes, I know her; in fact she should be with us in a few minutes, but why, what is the problem?" Charles selected his words carefully.

"Please tell me if you know a man called Khakkeki?"

Charles's mind went into overdrive. Now he really needed to select his words carefully; not to do so could be detrimental to Naomi's forthcoming interview with them. "No, I do not know a man called Khakkeki. But please sit down and we will wait for Naomi."

They entered the door and felt the cool air from the air conditioning and seemed to relax more; Charles even witnessed a smile from one of them.

There was an uneasy silence in the room as both parties did not want to weaken their hands. After about ten minutes they heard a taxi pull up outside.

Charles excused himself, walked outside and paid the driver, as he did so he lent over Naomi who whispered, "What are the police here for?"

"I am afraid it is you they want to question regarding Khakkeki." He looked at the ground to hide the movement of his lips from the police, who were observing them both from inside the house. "Look, Naomi, they want to know about your association with him."

"What will I say?"

"Then tell them the truth, my girl – but on second thoughts, advise them that he did not return to you, and you left before him. Which is the truth, isn't it?"

"Yes – I cannot lie, Charles, they will catch me out anyway if I do, and it will make it worse."

"If you do they will accuse you of not informing them; it will be difficult."

A pause in their conversation, then Naomi sighed. "Yes, I will say I was scared and left before Khakkeki came back."

They walked into the house and Naomi immediately approached the two policemen, and without a smile said coldly, "So you want to speak with me?"

"If you are Naomi Nzema, then yes, I do." Makobi introduced himself and his colleague. "Did you have an association with a man called Khakkeki?"

"He took me to a hotel against my will, and when he was called out on business I escaped and came home by taxi."

"Can you substantiate this?" asked the policeman.

"Yes," answered Naomi. "It was Leopold's Taxis, and the driver's name was Manda, the same as your friend here." She lied, as she had no chance of locating the old man who had offered her the lift.

"Mrs Nzema, the man you were with that evening was stabbed by a gang called Spots, and we now have positive proof that they are led by a businessman called Godfrey Ngosa. Unfortunately, Khakkeki got involved with Ngosa and owed him a substantial amount of money – this was the motive for his murder."

"He died? I knew he was in hospital but did not know... I am sorry."

"It was unfortunate, madam; he lasted two weeks before expiring." The policeman put on a sad face, then continued talking to Naomi. "We have been trying to arrest Ngosa for many months, but were unable to do so due to lack of evidence. But now we have that! Our only concern is that he lives in a house not more than eighty yards from where we are now, and will most certainly have some of his gang members with him, all of whom may be armed.

"At this stage we do not know how many men are living with him; it will be necessary for us to return with a warrant and an adequate band of armed officers to apprehend him. He is now wanted for murder in addition to money laundering, drug peddling and extortion; we will require you and Mr Charles to accompany us to the station for further verification."

"Are we under arrest?" asked Charles.

"No, sir, we are retaining you for your own protection. You are free to go if you want but it will be better if you come now to clarify the matter. We have already issued an arrest warrant for Ngosa, but we will require you both to testify."

Later that evening, a truck containing sixteen fully armed policemen drove within half a mile of Ngosa's house. Two officers were already in close proximity, maintaining contact with the officer in charge.

At precisely nine o'clock the superior officer stationed two men at each corner of the plot where Ngosa lived. They stretched out on the grass, trying to look inconspicuous, while the others approached the house directly from the front.

Only two of these, a senior policeman and an assistant, advanced to the porch and knocked. The maid answered and a conversation took place.

The team at the front of the house regrouped and stood discussing their next move. Suddenly a gunshot was heard at the rear of the house, and without exception the policemen hit the ground, their eyes wide and frightened.

There was silence – not a sound except the crickets. The whole team continued to lie still on the ground, then the commanding officer instructed four of them to make their way to the back of the house, he stayed under cover.

There they found two policemen, both standing rigid with rifles pointing at two men, one Ngosa and the other his aide, who was badly wounded and lying on the ground. Ngosa held his hands high, and did so until he was handcuffed and told to sit down. Two other men searched the house whilst the medic attended to the wounded man.

Seeing that the situation was now under control, the superior officer took the initiative and marched to the scene, where he barked an order to show his authority: "Chitoule, read them their rights, and get them off to the station. I will contact the director."

The man with his hands in the air was addressed by name. "Godfrey Ngosa, you are arrested on suspicion of murder, and anything that you say…"

After twenty minutes the two men searching the house returned and reported the all-clear. The maid and her husband were left to clean up, and feed the six policemen who were retained overnight. The rest of the squad returned to Head Office for a debriefing.

Charles and Naomi returned to Charles's home from the police station later that evening and settled down to watch his flickering black-and-white television set, their thoughts retracing an exciting day. Their conversation was lively as both were excited at the night's action and extremely relieved that Ngosa was behind bars and Naomi had been cleared of any wrongdoing at the hotel near Luanshya.

As they walked along the corridor to the bedroom, Naomi sighed. "At least the weight of that day with Khakkeki is all but cleared up. I am sorry that he died but I have a clear conscience."

Charles leant over and kissed her on the forehead. She had never experienced tenderness such as that this man had given her. It was not the African way, but she felt she needed Charles in her life; she would learn from him the ways of a gentleman and somehow return the tenderness he had expressed to her.

34

PEACE IN SIGHT, NOVEMBER 1981

It was now six months since the attempts on the lives of HM Queen Elizabeth and Pope John Paul II had taken place, and Irish politics was going through a major change.

Initially the atrocities carried out by the IRA during the 1970s brought about feelings of great antipathy from the public, but these were to soften. Those who vehemently opposed the IRA for their atrocities were now seeing another side to the passion of the nationalists, and attention was now focused on Maze Prison in Northern Ireland.

Bobby Sands, now a British MP, and six colleagues were in the Maze and dying on a hunger strike, putting their heads on the line in support of the cause.

On another front, Sinn Fein, the political side of the IRA, were making progress via peaceful negotiations in Parliament, and the fervour of change was in the air.

Sadly, Sands died in May 1981, his friends passed a few weeks later; it was a waste of young men's lives and with an end to hostilities clearly in sight.

Sinn Fein, the political wing of the IRA, had established a firm foothold and had taken their cause to the British and European Parliaments – at last a way forward to peace for the people of Northern Ireland. Times were changing and the power of the people was now a stronger force than the violence of previous years. The peace process was starting to bloom.

For the time being nothing had changed in the IRA's attitude or intent, and this would remain so until it was agreed formally; they had been foiled so many times in the past. It was an in-between time, both sides held by the leashes of political leaders, not knowing whether to attack or retreat.

But it was a time for retribution, too; not for the common soldier so much as the hated individuals who enjoyed the killing and harm they did to others. These individuals had committed extreme violence and were hated for their actions; their counterparts, on whichever side of the line they stood, took the liberty to take revenge where appropriate.

The IRA's business interests continued to thrive, raising money and procuring arms whenever possible. The Provisional Command Councils for each sector continued on a regular basis, and the fervour of rebellion remained on the agenda.

British Intelligence were also busy, and early in 1980 the joint surveillance of international intelligence agencies arrested the main source of IRA arms deals across the Atlantic. In view of the complexity and sophistication of these consignments, a seizure of arms was intercepted on the high seas. This was a clear indication that the IRA were not intending to halt operations just yet!

In the States and Canada the FBI were active and carried out raids on factories and storehouses, and coastguards on both sides of the Atlantic were kept busy.

After the terrible incident that occurred at Narrow Water Castle the Royal Ulster Constabulary introduced a special unit, trained by the SAS in Hereford to SAS standards. This team had its own cruel principles and work ethic; it was to take on the IRA on its own terms. The small unit went by the strange title of E4A, and soon after it was formed the actions it carried out were thought to be outside the boundaries of reasonable law. It was disbanded shortly afterwards.

'Shoot now and ask questions later' appeared to be their motto, and their actions were never opposed by the RUC, who always stood up to defend them. Many accusations followed, with stern allegations from the nationalists that collusion existed between MI5, the RUC and the British military regarding a huge military cover-up. It then transpired that if the E4A were ever to be prosecuted it would reveal too many classified activities; the government closed down the unit.

McGirk, commander of the South Armagh division of the IRA, had called a special meeting that was to be held in a secret location. The exact location would not be disclosed until the day of the meeting.

It was the responsibility of his second in command, a man called O'Rierdan, to ensure all appropriate people attended. The invitation list was distributed to eight of McGirk's lieutenants; the invitations included all the necessary information with the exception of the location, which would be issued the day before they travelled.

O'Donnell, the first to arrive at Ferron's Farm, knocked on the large, old door. He was already complaining of the manure on his shoes; he'd parked his car inside an old pigsty. "Bloody farms always have this smell and mess everywhere; I will never get the stench out of my clothes," he murmured to himself.

The door opened and a small, elderly man stood before him. He was balding, and greeted O'Donnell with a wide, toothless grin. "Come in, come in, Danny. It is good to see you, you are the first to arrive, to be sure you are."

"Thank you, Thomas; it is good to see you too, but you must keep that bloody yard of yours clean, it is filthy."

Thomas laughed and patted the cushions on one of the chairs, indicating for O'Donnell to sit down. "Now I'll get you a cup of tea, and if there is a knock on the door, let them in; they always come when I am not here."

Whilst the host was in the kitchen the door was opened three times, and within a few minutes of Thomas returning with the tea the remaining four members of the brigade were in the house, talking amongst themselves.

McGirk called for order. Sufficient time had passed for all to be ready, and on this note Thomas left the room, shutting the door behind him. He knew approximately how long the meeting would take, so sauntered up the hill to the highest point of his small farm. To walk to this point took him fifteen minutes, so once he got there he lit his pipe and, with his elbows on the fence, gazed out over the fields below.

After the meeting was called to order, McGirk, a religious man, said a short prayer. Some paid attention and others didn't, but they all finished the prayer in unison, saying, "Amen."

"I have some news that we will discuss, then we'll go on to review each and every man's work brief over the next two months. The actions are not all tedious; they are, however, necessary due to the 'peace' process that is currently being debated by our friends the politicians. We will continue our duties as necessary.

"I would stress that we have lost some valuable consignments over the last month and our leaders feel that this is due to a grass amongst us. It is necessary that we all do not discuss anything within the brigade unless I am in attendance.

"Our arguments with our British friends are not over yet; it is too early to retire with our esteemed political party still negotiating."

The IRA members all sat quietly on the old wooden dining chairs, waiting for the preliminaries to stop, so the more important actions regarding delegation and magnitude could be discussed.

McGirk summed up the past and present situation. "During 1979 and 1980 the brigade was busy. We had a lot of success against the Brits, but the old way of negotiating seems to be slipping into the past; a change is coming and we need to move with the times, support our leaders, keep loyal to the flag."

He looked down at his notes briefly and went on. "The hits that we as a brigade were involved with went according to plan, perhaps too well, so much so that the media have made it 'bad reading'. It has tarnished our reputation and we have lost many sympathisers, and that has in turn impacted our sponsors' generosity.

"The Maze prisoners, our brothers, continue to battle with the authorities and we send our prayers to the boys who sacrificed themselves in the face of adversity; we will support them no matter what.

"Sinn Fein is making tremendous steps forward politically and our case is now on track for a United Ireland, although I for one do not trust Westminster; the British have a bad track record for making promises and breaking them.

He paused and threw in a word of caution. "If politics does not sort out our problems and allow us to govern Ireland as we want, our times will remain as dangerous as they are now. We will maintain our posts and business deals, continue to build our reserves, and none of you will change a thing until I tell you so. But for now we will do little and wait for further instructions from our leader, and we will call another general meeting in three months from now."

The attendees got up from their seats and made for the kitchen; it seemed that this was the best place to discuss business. It was much larger than the living room, and Thomas had returned from his walk and was setting up the table with plates of food and plenty of bottles of alcohol.

"So now our brigade is becoming obsolete, we can have a game of golf. It will certainly replace these intense meetings; how times have changed." John O'Halloran addressed the two colleagues he was drinking with at the bar.

"Perhaps," answered the man next to him. "Let's see what happens, but it will be a first if we can control all of Ireland. At worst it will end with a power-sharing arrangement, but we will have to wait and see."

After the meal was over and the team were bonding, Thomas returned for his walk up the hill and he scanned the countryside with binoculars, it was all clear and he walked back and opened the door one at a time before the leaders were on their way.

Barney Coughlin was not given a mention.

35

A WOMAN SCORNED, NOVEMBER 1981

The group of elderly ladies had changed their venue for their monthly meeting. They were all seated in George's Café in Marylebone, and were doing what all elderly ladies do: chatting. Most of the time it was worthless rubbish to everyone else but those ladies present.

The ladies met on a regular basis and the lateness of one of their members did not deter them in the slightest, they just continued exchanging useless gossip of no importance then to themselves. The lady in question would have been early but for a thought – something was troubling her. On instinct, she turned back for home, and did not give her visit another thought. Six months previously, Barney Coughlin, a one-time IRA terrorist, had come into her life. She had developed feelings for him, and then he left her, but this did not trouble her as much the bad deeds he did before leaving her home: he had wronged her, disrespected her deceased husband, and whilst doing this had carried out an illegal action. She had been deceived by his charm and subsequently he had abandoned her, an older woman left unwanted by a younger man. She was irate and felt used; it was time to settle this with the law.

What was more disturbing for her was the fact that he had taken her late husband's identity. At first she wasn't sure; it was apparent she had serious emotions for him, it was not about her feelings as much as the illegality that surrounded his actions, it was her opinion as she saw them with hindsight.

He had related to her a tale of intrigue and his classified IRA training; she wasn't even sure whether this was an honest admission or just another lie he had told her.

She shivered – her thoughts were disturbing. He was an enemy of the British government, and if his story was true then how many innocent people had been killed on his account? She needed to share this information, whether it was with the police or the Diplomatic Corps. She picked up the phone and dialled a Paddington number.

"Officer, I may be ringing the wrong people but I would like to speak with someone regarding misrepresentation of a person I became involved with."

"Yes, ma'am – can I first start with your name and address? We can then arrange a date and time for you to come to the station, or if that is not convenient then perhaps we can arrange to meet at your home."

"Sarah Siddons, I am a widow." She went on to advise the policeman of her address.

"Do you wish to come here to the station, or is your home more convenient?"

"The station is fine, Officer."

"May I suggest three o'clock today?"

"Yes, I will be there."

"That's fine, Mrs Siddons; I will arrange to have an officer interview you, and he will know the next step to take."

She made her way home, and started to prepare for her meeting.

Her meeting with an Inspector Wilton was intense and she felt that she had answered without total fluency; it was as if the inspector was challenging everything she said. He made a phone call, talked for a few moments and then returned his attention to Sarah.

"What you have told me is very interesting and the details concerning our friend Coughlin are of course illegal, so I have discussed your situation with the Intelligence Service and they have arranged to send a man down from Head Office. He will be here to talk with you in approximately thirty minutes."

"Do I have to stay here?" asked Sarah.

"Yes, ma'am, we would appreciate it, so please take a seat in the room over there and we will make you a cup of tea and a sandwich."

It was forty minutes later that a very well-dressed man entered the room. He smiled, although this told Sarah nothing; his eyes had been cold when he entered the room and remained so now. He moved to a chair adjacent to where Sarah was sitting. "May I sit?"

"Yes, of course," answered Sarah.

"Now, Mrs Siddons, my name is Bill Dean. I work for HM Intelligence Service, and I would appreciate it if, in your own time, you could tell me everything about this situation that you find yourself in."

Two hours later, she left the police station, exhausted, and walked back to her home near Paddington Station.

After escorting Sarah to the door and bidding her goodbye, Dean picked up the telephone and dialled a number.

"Hello, Webster here."

"George, it's me, Dean."

"Yes, Bill?"

"I have finished my interview with Mrs Siddons and you will be interested in our discussion regarding Coughlin, our long-lost Irish terrorist."

"I will be very interested, so I suggest, Bill, that you ring your wife and inform her that you will be home late, is that OK?"

"OK, that is fine with me, George. See you soon."

THE EVENING AFTER

George Webster pondered on the conversation he'd had with Bill Dean the evening before. He knew it was important in allocating the appropriate time and resource in endeavouring to locate Coughlin. The man was now more a nuisance than a threat but he still needed to be found, and it was his responsibility to do it.

Which direction would the Irishman take? George had tracked him as far as Africa but now his whereabouts were official he would need to start from the beginning.

The first and most important question was, where would a fugitive head for if he wanted to lie low without too much efficiency from the local security?

Europe he thought too close; the States and Canada could be possibilities, especially if Coughlin became involved with the underworld? George's first lead may come from either border control or the ticket sales agencies. But if Coughlin already had a new identity this approach would be useless – unless, of course, he had used Charles Siddons' passport or his credit card. That would make George's life a lot easier. It would be difficult to trace a pedestrian on the ferries, unless a ticket had been bought with a credit card.

George thought hard. His first instincts told him Coughlin was still in Africa and would pursue the path he had already taken. A huge continent, one where a fugitive could easily get lost among a mass of people, where corruption was endemic, and an easy place to hide.

He set up a special meeting with his team and included some others who were specialists in the task in question.

The situation regarding Coughlin was now a nuisance factor; Webster had higher priorities and Coughlin may at this stage be more trouble than he was worth. He had defrauded a lady who seemed to have a romantic grudge against the Irishman, and this had now developed into a possible legal complaint. A clear case of alleged terrorism was now a messy situation that involved fraud and misrepresentation.

He had set his team to work on highest-priority items, of which the Coughlin affair was not one, but he would persevere during the next few days and hope that something would break on the situation.

Three days later he recalled his team to review the situation.

"Guys, what do we have?"

The team produced a report that listed the place where sightings were evident although they were all unconfirmed.

There was one on Ancona-Split ferry, another from Irish ferries and another from the Tarifa-Tangier ferry.

The most promising was the Irish ferries where it was said a group of men all but one was the worse for drink, and it was this particular individual that resembled Coughlin's profile.

It was reported that a ticket had been bought with cash at a kiosk near Gibraltar. The buyer was Irish and the ferry was to Tangier, but again, this was unconfirmed.

Mike Nottage, an MI6 agent covering the Africa region, asked George, "Didn't you have a contact in Africa? I was under the impression you spoke with him recently; perhaps he would know something? You know how expatriates stick together."

George stiffened and sat upright. "Yes, that's right, Mike, I do. Although he is on the Copperbelt in Zambia, it is always worth a call, and come to think of it, he has been, er, vacant of late."

That evening George tried many times to get through to Martin but the phone just rang out. After the third time he gave up, intending to ring again during the next few days.

Little did he know that further perseverance might have given him the information he was after.

36

AT A LOW EBB

It seemed that both Charles and Naomi had exhausted all their ideas. Their resources were dwindling, all their contacts proved unhelpful, but they remained resolute, and he promised to commit to finding her children, whatever disappointments they may face on the way.

Charles was beginning to be concerned with the outcome regarding his meeting with Martin, and it would be necessary to advise Naomi of any bad news that may arise in the future. Subsequently he explained to her the recent events and the possible outcome of his meeting, although he felt that she did not understand the full implications; they seemed of secondary importance to her. She had listened to everything he had said but it never entered her head that anyone in their right mind would arrest Charles; he was just too considerate, a perfect gentleman – nothing was going to happen to him!

The following day Martin informed Charles that he was aware of his identity theft, and how this information had become known to MI6. It was, said Martin, "the anger of a woman scorned".

Charles continued to play golf and his friendships with his friends grew, although it seemed Martin was pulling back. Charles was not sure whether this was because of his outside business or his unwillingness to continue mixing with a known fraudster.

All things in life seem to happen at the worst moment, and on this particular day it happened to Martin.

He had worked an exhausting day at the mines and found his evenings invaluable; this was his time to ensure that the boxers were in their best shape for the upcoming show at the trade fair.

Rushing home, he grabbed a sandwich, pulled on his training suit and made his way to the door. It was then that the telephone rang, he thought that it always seemed to ring at the last moment, he thought of ignoring it, but changed direction and lifted the receiver. "Hello, who is it?"

"Martin, you seem annoyed – everything all right, old chap?"

"Everything is fine, George, but I am in a hurry to get out; got something on."

"Anything important?" George was trying to be polite.

"Not really – I have signed the second stage of the contract required for the next show. Martin was showing irritation.

"Nothing really, but just a heads-up – it's about our friend Coughlin."

"What about him?" Martin wanted to get away, but needed to know the gossip.

"Well, apart from being a former IRA bomber, it seems that Coughlin has stolen someone's identity, and the deceased man's wife is not happy, he has utilised the dead man's bank account but this access is now closed. The police are involved and I for one need to locate him."

"Thanks, George, but he hasn't turned up here, and if he does I will certainly contact you." Martin felt a tingle of disgust as he lied openly.

He wanted to end the call and move on; he was late and now annoyed, but he carried on the conversation under duress. "You know, George, although Africa is huge, gossip travels for miles; the travelling fraternity exchange news quite inexplicably in this part of the world. If he gets within a hundred miles of here we will know and I will pass on the information."

"I understand, Martin. Sorry for repeating myself. I will let you go, but ring me even if you hear only a peep."

"OK, George."

Martin replaced the phone, and was out of the door in a flash. He hoped that he had not been too brusque with George, and he did feel a hint of guilt.

SARAH'S PREDICAMENT

Sarah Siddons felt better. She had got matters off her chest with the police and they in turn had helped her straighten things out with her affairs. She had capped Barney's access to her deceased husband's accounts and the use of his passport was terminated.

She was not totally convinced that her actions reflected what she really wanted. She still had feelings for Barney, but out of respect for her husband, Charles's memory did not warrant any association she might have had with an IRA agent.

Once again, her life became mundane: her weekly meeting's with her friends was not stimulating enough, she clearly felt that someone else was taken from her.

37

IN NEW YORK, NOVEMBER 1981

Hugh McGirk was agitated. It seemed that his organisation was in turmoil – had all those years of conflict been wasted? The dreams of an integrated Ireland governed by the Irish were fading into the past. He began to wonder if the current political situation would ever resolve the differences between unionists and nationalists.

His senior, the IRA chief of staff, had made it clear that there would be no let-up in hostilities with the British until Sinn Fein had a firm political foothold in both the European Parliament and the Northern Ireland Assembly. McGirk had noted that the chief of staff had stood down prior to the Assembly elections. It seemed he had other things on his mind – perhaps a step into the political forum?

The army council up to this time had been kept busy by the prevailing friction that was pursued by both sides. There was a violent tit-for-tat between nationalists and unionists, and this escalated with the hunger strikes in Maze Prison during the spring of 1981. In support of the strikers the IRA retaliated with a symbolic assassination of a prominent unionist, but during this action an innocent caretaker was also killed. As unfortunate as it was for the caretaker, the beginning of the end of hostilities in Northern Ireland was becoming a realistic prospect, with both sides starting to come to their senses.

A common factor in this game of war had been car bombings, but now even those seemed to be a thing of the past. It was necessary that agents from both sides maintained discipline; what was not wanted at this stage of the peace talks was an overexuberant member overstepping the mark and taking military action without permission.

The IRA had grown up over the years, from a clumsy novice into a highly efficient organisation. They continued to plan for war and there would be no let-up for the time being, and they continued to procure expensive armaments that would warn the British that they still meant business.

A good example of their intent occurred in the 1980s when the IRA spent two million pounds on a single deal. This consignment consisted of many sophisticated items, including ground-to-air missiles, bomb-carrying drones, and automatic assault weapons. It was an expensive business, and because of the huge costs involved the expenditure needed to be controlled carefully against income. There were also other costs that needed to be accounted for, including salaries for unemployed members, car purchases, safe houses, propaganda and party election campaign expenses, and these too needed to be balanced against income. An impressive range of methods helped to maintain this balance of payments, including tax fraud, protection rackets, gambling machines, pubs, taxis, and a reliable income from the many Irish organisations around the US that collected from the public on a continual basis.

There is one character that appears in any major conflict. The defector, the supergrass or the rat – whatever name they go by, they are loathed by those they work with. Their duties are despised and cast a shadow over normal soldiers; they leave behind a stench called distrust; they sell their soul. It is a sinister side of war and in Northern Ireland at this time it was no different; there were defectors on both sides who conspired against their own kind.

In the Provisional IRA the grass, or more appropriately the rat, sells his information for money and will ask for immunity for turning in Queen's evidence. But being a grass is dangerous: if found out, there is no mercy, and they expect their end to be more than painful.

Crime in the IRA is categorised into four groups: petty, serious, rape, and crimes against the IRA punishable by death. The latter applies to the supergrass.

Of the punishments themselves, some are grotesque and too hideous to mention. One particular method made famous during the Troubles was that of 'kneecapping'. The victim was identified and taken to some desolate place. They would be stretched out on the ground and the next stage of punishment depended on the seriousness of the crime. For a minor offence the victim would be shot through the thigh, then he was shot through the back of the knee, then through the backs of both knees, and if the crime was judged to be serious, the victim was shot through both knees and both elbow joints.

As life became more civilised in the 1980s this type of punishment was dropped from the agenda. The supergrass situation was prevalent on both sides during the Troubles, but became even more prolific when the end was in sight and retribution loomed.

If a disclosure by a grass was not corroborated after he had turned Queen's evidence, the IRA called an amnesty. In this way the grass's stories would be withdrawn and useless to the prosecution. The family of the grass would be in the line of fire.

In 1984 Sinn Fein were making good progress but were still novices in politics. This was apparent when they did not understand why the votes for the European Parliament in 1983 were much greater in number than those collected for the Northern Ireland general election a year later. This phenomenon was diagnosed as 'the unreality of expectations'.

Ironically, within the European Parliament, Northern Ireland was regarded as one constituency with only three seats. They realised that their political fight must be carried out on a much broader front than first anticipated, although the setback was only temporary. There were other ways in which the nationalists could wield the power they yearned for.

Sinn Fein were still trying to make their mark and were experiencing problems on the political front, but it was nothing compared to what their IRA brothers were experiencing whilst trying to procure arms at the sharp end of the campaign. On both sides of the Atlantic the USA/Canadian satellite surveillance team were closely monitoring the illegal arms trade, and they had identified two ships from the US crossing the Atlantic allegedly carrying arms. These two separate consignments were to anchor inshore off the coast of Ireland and transfer their arms to another ship, but the British authorities were tipped off and the vessels intercepted and their consignments destroyed.

McGirk was aware of this situation. He was also smarting after the failure of his brigade's operation in the Shetlands. He was a man who wanted success, and failure was not an option.

Personally, he wanted to put things right. Perhaps another hit would make him feel better? It would satisfy his ego, and may also quicken up the politicians at Stormont.

Both sides were sparring politically, each trying to sway the public and get a sympathy vote. Bobby Sands and his colleagues had made the ultimate sacrifice; they died for their beliefs. It was a sad waste of human life, and even more so that this should happen so close to the peace talks. Maze Prison was not big enough for Sands and his friends, and through a peaceful demonstration that hurt no one but themselves, using no bombs or guns, they died for what they believed in. It captured the public's imagination, and they earned sympathy the hard way.

McGirk drew a deep breath and stared far out of his window, deep in thought. It did not take him long to come to a conclusion, and he picked up the phone and rang his wife.

"Hello, dear, it's me, Hugh. Don't pack the bags; we will stay a bit longer, in fact much longer. I will be home shortly."

BACK IN THE HOME TOWN, MAY 1982

The Irish reporters were no longer working overtime; the newspapers did not contain the sensationalism that had existed in the 1970s. It was now down to mundane politics.

Barney and his oldest friend Declan had known each other since childhood. They grew up together and joined the IRA for the same reasons. They had expected to become Republican heroes, but things had not turned out as they wanted, with Barney absconding from the army after losing his belief in their methods, leaving his friend to fend for himself. Declan did try and maintain momentum but failed in the eyes of the IRA and was captured by the security forces whilst making his escape from Shetland.

The biggest change in Declan's personal life was the termination of his association with his long-term girlfriend Bridget McClory. It seemed the right thing to do; after all, his life was one of risk and for this reason he did not want Bridget to be tied to him.

It was after his internment in Wandsworth that he began to think of her often. He was feeling alone and vulnerable, and he wanted his girl back.

In November 1981 he was transferred to Maze Prison near Belfast and resumed contact with her by letter. She did not visit him there, and had tried to sever all association with him after he disappeared without so much as a goodbye.

As time went on and his story became public, she softened and even felt sympathy for him. She had remained single since his departure, not out of any feelings for him, but for the sake of their child, born nine months after Declan had left her. Since his arrest in May 1981 they had exchanged letters but she had never mentioned the child he had fathered.

Bridget was Declan's love, and Barney his best friend, and they filled his mind from morning to night. He wanted to know how his friend was. Where was he? Had he survived?

He did not get many visitors; it seemed his friends and relatives had deserted him. If only he knew what had happened to Barney...

THE WALL, 1985

In Russia the turmoil within the rural communities was becoming untenable. The people were growing restless; their collective strength greater. The old communist regime was teetering; Lenin had played his part and Stalin had destroyed it with his brutality.

Students are always at the centre of public dissent, and in 1980s Russia it was no different. The country was at the point of a revolution and Mikhail Gorbachev, the president-elect, was standing in the wings, ready to change history.

38

THE TRADE FAIR,
MARCH 1982

Agricultural fairs are held in rural areas the world over. Initially established in medieval Europe, they have spread beyond all borders; where there is farming, there is a show. All over the globe farmers and associated companies market their wares; the trade fair is a platform of convenience, a way to show off commodities for sale, whether they are market equipment, animals or sport.

The large agricultural stadium in Kitwe is sectionalised from the show grounds. It has its own access roads, a dedicated main entrance with ticket kiosk, huge terracing, and high-powered electrical facilities with control room.

On a normal day, with the place deserted, the sun beating down, and wind and dust in your face, the stadium feels uninteresting, not worth a second look. But in the cool of the evening, with lights blazing, a buzz from the crowd, the roar of ten thousand fans, animation and happiness in their faces, it becomes a sight to enjoy.

The show comes but once a year. It takes place in May, and the floats are individually sponsored, decorated according to a theme and manned by hundreds of children. For them and thousands of others it is a special time.

Martin was concerned that, because his show was last on the Saturday schedule, any delay ahead of him would have a major impact, and he knew from previous experience that this was almost certain to happen. He decided to make arrangements so that this would not happen here; he could not deny his ten thousand fans.

Martin's philosophy was to eliminate any risk before it began, anything that was seen to be a problem, and if this meant making a 'dash' at the right time to the right person, then so be it.

Any event held in Africa draws interest from anyone with power, especially if they can get something free, and promotions are no different. If it is an event that carries any esteem and is close to towns with good hotels the event will attract government officials that can take their girlfriends or boyfriends and get a good weekend at the promoters expense. They travelled from Lusaka with a guest and expected accommodation, meals and free entrance to the show. This was a request he could not refuse; it might attract trouble that he wanted to avoid, but for him it creates a lot of unnecessary expense against the shows budget.

He did this to safeguard against any government interference, but now he wanted payback and would approach those who accepted his invitation after their receipt of their tickets and hotel confirmation.

Now with the show still a couple of months away, Martin planned another holiday with his golfing friends to Zimbabwe.

Early in March the four golfers, including the impossible duo of Martin and Charles, set off to Victoria Falls. It was a ten-hour journey and they hoped that Martin and Charles might find the trip as a way to bond a little. Jim, who was using his company Mercedes, drove them.

They stopped on the Zambian side of the Falls and found accommodation in an old guest house. The rooms and bedding were spotless, the floors scrubbed so you could see your face in them. They rose early, the sun's rays breaking through the skylight window and onto the breakfast table, and sat down for a modest but satisfying meal. Afterwards they drove to the Livingstone Golf Club, only a few hundred yards from the guesthouse where they were staying.

Their first game was entertaining mainly because none of the players had previously experienced these particular conditions. The fairways were sparse, the grass having lost its battle with the hot sun. But approaching the first green they were confused as the flag was visible but the greens were not what they were used to. Only 'oiled sand' confronted them, putting was almost impossible, and a roller was required to smooth the sand after each putt.

After the game they asked the club professional if this was normal and he told them that indeed it was in this part of the world. He added that Elephant Hills did have greens but a round would be three times as expensive as at the Livingstone.

The Rhodesian Civil War occurred between 1964 and 1979, finishing a year and a bit before the golfers decided to play at Elephant Hills. The war was a complicated, triangular affair that involved the predominantly white government of Ian Smith, the African National Congress, and the People's Revolutionary Army. It was basically a civil war made more complicated by the tribal situation between the latter two groups.

After years of fighting commanders-in-chiefs signed a peace deal after the cessation of hostilities in March 1980; this occurred at the Lancaster Hotel in London far away from the place of war.

Those that signed the deal were Ian Smith (government), Robert Mugabe (ANC) and Joshua Nkomo (PRA).

The actual handover to the new ruling party took place in 1982 almost two years after the initial peace deal was signed.

Even between the elections and the final peace agreement in 1980, a number of incidents occurred, one of which affected the four golfers about to play at Elephant Hills.

Three months prior to the final peace agreement, the ANC fired a ground-to-air missile at an enemy aircraft flying low over Elephant Hills Golf Course. The missile, a heat-seeking device, locked on to the aircraft's engines, but was diverted suddenly and instead picked up heat rising from the golf course kitchen. When the dust settled the bomb had wiped out the clubhouse, and killed nine people. Renovations were delayed due to lack of funds, and a temporary clubhouse was installed in the interim.

The golfers enjoyed their weekend and the Falls looked magnificent; the spray from the water rising to the viewing points. Apart from encountering a spitting cobra who did not appreciate the four of them blocking his path as they strolled around the periphery of the Falls, nothing untoward happened.

However, the most valued memory of their visit was the bonding between Martin and Charles. Even the eight-hour return trip could not devalue this.

There was a downside to the holiday, and it came from an unexpected source.

Jim, who worked for a Kitwe fabrication contractor, had used his company car for the trip, but this was seen by competitors to be a gift in return for commercial favours. Brendan and Martin were both clients and Jim had provided them with a holiday; it seemed a minor oversight when the situation first arose, but blew up totally out of proportion.

After an enquiry Jim was released from his duties and flew back to the UK a few weeks later.

39

A SURPRISE, JANUARY 1982

Just after Christmas in 1982, Martin received a call from the MI6 agent George Webster.

"Hello, Martin, long time since we spoke last, although I did try and contact you before Christmas."

"Yes, I missed you and totally forgot to ring you back; my apologies."

Martin now realised he needed to be guarded in what he said with respect to his friendship with Charles.

"Martin, our man Barney Coughlin – you will recall when we spoke last we discussed Coughlin had secured a new identity and obtained it by fraud ?"

"Hold up, George, either I am getting too old and have forgotten this conversation or you have made a mistake!"

"Well, either way we need to take a different tack with this man."

"In what way?"

"He is now a fraudster as well as a terrorist and cheated an unsuspecting widow of many thousands of pounds."

"Thanks for that, George, but I don't know what you want from me; this guy may be anywhere in the world, and I certainly do not expect him to pop up in this little part of Africa."

"I know, but news travels faster in the bush by word of mouth than by the bloody telephone. All I am asking is that you please keep your eyes and ears open for any information on him. He is fading from the terrorist scene and now unimportant to most, but he is still my call. I was given the responsibility of finding him, and after I do so, I want to close his file for good."

"OK, George, I fully understand and take your point, and will do my best to keep my ear to the ground. If I hear something, I will be on the phone to you."

"Thanks, Martin; hope to hear from you soon, then." As George put down the phone he had the feeling that there had been an icy edge to Martin's tone.

Martin did not feel at all guilty regarding the discussions with the MI6 man and earnestly packed his bags. He was off on a jaunt with Wolfgang, who had invited him to experience bush life, eating, drinking and sleeping under the stars; a weekend to enjoy. The German loved his bush jaunts and planned them to perfection, taking everything bar the kitchen sink.

The arrangements for travel for the trip were made with precise German organisation.

Wolfgang was taking two vehicles, one a large Toyoto bakkie. It was big enough to fit his deep freezer, and two of his factory workers in the rear section that was open; the two workers had volunteered for the trip and would benefit from the fish they caught and any game meat that went spare. Apart from Wolfgang who would drive, everything else would be stored in the open loading section at the back.

The second vehicle was a Saab estate: this would be driven by Wolfgang's foreman, a man called Helmut and he would drive with Martin as the passenger, with bedding stored on the back seat.

The Toyota carried guns, fishing rods and other utensils required whilst the Saab carried all things that were to keep dry in case of rain.

The Toyoto would also pull Wolfgang's small motorboat as he intended to show Martin the excitement that can be had catching Tiger fish on the Zambezi.

Wolfgang acquired a yearly hunting licence that allowed him to legally kill five game animals a year. When the animals were killed they were dismembered to fit into the fridge-freezer in the back of his truck and taken back to Kitwe for his family to eat.

The two Africans came for the experience and any opportunity to catch fish and edible insects. The fish they caught would be cleaned, dried, salted and stored for the future.

Martin accepted the invitation as an adventure, a chance to see Africa and its animals in their own habitat, to taste and smell the bush, and to sleep under the stars and experience the dangers that lingered in every corner.

He did not expect what was to be the outcome.

Over the campfire one evening, Martin told a story to Wolfgang and Helmut and explained why he would never carry a gun or anything else that would hurt an animal. It occurred when he was young and killed a bird with his catapult. The bird dropped into the waters of a river in front of him; it was a simple action but he felt it was not his duty to hurt living creatures without a reason, and he stuck to his vow.

They looked at him in astonishment, then at each other, and then shrugged. Nothing more was said on the matter.

A day before they were due to return, an accident occurred that was to cast a cloud over the trip and delay their return by two days.

Wolfgang had not 'culled' any animals since they arrived; his freezer was empty and he needed to make a kill for the meat.

They had spent most of the time on the Zambezi catching fish and lost track of time for actual hunting.

The next day they took just one vehicle, the bakkie, with Wolfgang and Martin in the front and Helmut, John and Abe, the two Africans, in the back.

After finding a suitable area to park, they trekked the bush, forming a straight line, moving slowly and inspecting every bush and tree. Wolfgang was leading with his gun held high, and Helmut brought up the rear, his gun cocked but pointing skyward.

Passing a group of trees, they spotted three buffalo grazing upstream of the wind at a distance of about fifty yards. Wolfgang raised his arm for the group to stop, then moved on towards the animals with John, the tall African, about five yards behind him.

Within about thirty-five yards of the beast, Wolfgang lifted his gun slowly and fired. The buffalo nearest to him seemed to be hit, but ran into the bush behind the others on hearing the shot. With caution Wolfgang walked towards where he thought the buffalo were resting. As he edged forward, John moved stealthily to join him but Wolfgang waved him back. Suddenly all hell was let loose. The injured beast broke loose from behind the high bush; it was breathing heavily and roaring. It lumbered towards the hunters, who by this time had almost reached the tree just ahead of the animal, and then John, standing close to Wolfgang, was hauled into the air by the buffalo and fell heavily to the ground. Wolfgang was within feet of the huge, steaming animal, and in a second raised his gun and fired. The bull shuddered, and steam and body parts scattered in the air as it fell to the ground.

The other three had by this time beaten all speed records over fifty yards and were now peering over the back fender of the bakkie. Immediately after the bull was felled they leapt from the cover of the vehicle and rushed towards the stricken John, who was screaming on the ground – the shock had worn off. Wolfgang was already attending to his left leg when they reached him; it was almost detached at the knee.

Wolfgang instructed Helmut to bring the bakkie close, and Martin and Abe to hold John still whilst Wolfgang laid his legs side by side. Helmut brought the bakkie as instructed, and handed Wolfgang the medical kit; he wrapped tape around both legs and injected the felled lad with morphine.

Gently he was lifted into the bakkie and Wolfgang drove him in the direction of the field hospital; it was thought to be over twenty miles away.

After nightfall Wolfgang returned in a sombre mood and informed the team that the lad had lost his leg below the knee. They would return home without him, and he would return by ambulance later.

40

A MESSAGE,
APRIL 1982

Naomi arrived home one evening to find a letter from her uncle in Maputo. It was unusual for him to write, so she was especially interested in the contents.

He had visited a church in the parish of Chingola a few miles from where Naomi lived, and met a Ghanaian lady who knew Naomi from her time with Kwasi, and she thought she might be able to help in locating the children.

Naomi wasted no time, she quickly wrote the lady's contact details and armed with the lady's business address, jumped on a bus and headed to Chingola.

It was a hectic bus ride from Kitwe, and she was disappointed to find that the lady was at a meeting and not available, so she waited for an hour. When the lady finally arrived Naomi recognised her from the Ghanaian parties she and Kwasi had attended in Kitwe.

"My name is Mary. It is a pleasure to meet with you again after so many years, and I am sorry that you broke with Kwasi but I understand the situation; he was a naughty boy."

"Yes, he was," answered Naomi. "But please tell me what you know of the situation now."

"Well, I know that he was here in Chingola not more than a week ago, and stayed at a house in Embele Street, and I think he was with one of the children, although I did not see him whilst he was here." Mary looked at Naomi and shrugged.

"What number was it in Embele Street?" Naomi asked.

"Number 2, it is the first house on the right-hand side."

"I will try to see if he is still there. Thank you, Mary, for your help." Naomi set off to find the house.

In the meantime Charles had arrived at Naomi's apartment in Kitwe saw the note and decided to follow her, but first he rang the number on the note that Naomi had left.

"Hello, I am trying to locate my friend Naomi Zimba. Have you seen her?" Charles asked politely.

"Yes, she was here but I sent her to Embele street, No 2, she is looking for ex-husband."

"How do you know he is at the address? Did you see him?"

"No, I did not see him, but I heard through the community that he was there just a week or so ago. That's all." She could not tell him anything more.

"How long ago was she with you, madam?"

"One hour, sir."

"If you see her then tell her I am on my way." He ended the call and then rang for a taxi.

Naomi reached the address. The house seemed badly maintained, and sitting on the front porch were three unkempt middle-aged local men, drinking from cans of beer.

Only one, the most grotesque, acknowledged her, and raised his eyebrows. "What can I do for you?"

The situation seemed wrong, and she recoiled. It reminded her of the time with Khakkeki.

"I need to speak with the lady of the house. If she is not here, I will come back later." She kept her distance, but in an effort to extract some information from the men, she went straight to the point. "What can you tell me regarding Kwasi Nzema?"

"Why do you want to know about Kwasi?"

"He was my husband, and I am trying to locate my three children."

"Is he the guy from Ghana?" asked the man.

"Yes."

"You were married to him? Well, well." The man laughed.

Naomi glared at him. "If he was here, did he have my children?"

"He might have, but if you want any more information it will cost you."

"Cost me what?"

"Wait; I will get a letter I have from him, and if you want the address, I will sell it to you." He got up and waddled through the door of the house. "Come, my daughter will make us a cup of tea."

She did not follow immediately, but at the mention of his daughter she moved towards the house.

The inside of the house was more orderly; the floor tiles were polished and the walls painted white, and there were a few chairs positioned around a small television set, and some glasses on a table in the middle of the room.

She waited at the door and shouted, "Have you found the letter?"

"My daughter is searching for it. Come in and wait."

She moved closer to the door and edged about a yard inside. He was sitting in a huge armchair, and had opened a beer and was drinking it from the neck of the bottle.

"My wife is out shopping; she is originally from Accra and will discuss Kwasi with you when she returns."

"Where is your daughter?"

"She is in the bedroom." He motioned towards the door to another room.

He got up from the chair and poured two whiskies from a bottle on the sideboard. He offered Naomi one but she refused.

"Come, woman, forget and have a drink; we will live a little."

"Your daughter is not here, is she?" Naomi raised her voice.

"Why worry about my daughter?" he laughed. "She must have gone shopping as well."

"Then I must go." Naomi hesitated.

The fat man was now sitting on the edge of his chair. His elbows were on his knees and the whisky glass between his legs. "Hold it; I may be able to find something out. Just wait and I will make a phone call."

She moved to the window and collected her thoughts. *Perhaps he can find something out?*

Her thoughts got the better of her and she turned to leave, but he surprised her and grabbed her by the shoulders and tried to kiss her. His strong arms were around her waist and his whisky breath almost choked her. She screamed and pulled away, but as she did so their legs entwined and they fell heavily to the floor.

She gasped at him, "Get away from me, you beast," and climbed to her feet.

He had one hand on her leg, and the other grabbed her skirt.

"Let me go, man!"

"We fuck!" he blurted. His hand moved round and grabbed the back of her panties.

"Get off me!" she screamed, and managed to move into a crouch, then, with a huge push of her legs, straightened up into a standing position. The man fell back onto the floor, but he still gripped her leg and she winced in pain.

He levered himself up, using her body to do so. She punched him in the face; his lip was now bleeding and, in trying to balance himself, he spread his legs. He was now in a position to hit her back, but before he could do anything she sunk her teeth into his neck, and he screamed loud profanities. A heavy man, he swung a massive arm that hit her high on the head and she was hurled across the room.

Victorious, he looked at the girl lying on the floor, her clothes askew. He unzipped the flies of his trousers and moved towards her fallen body. Now only half conscious, she moaned and turned onto her side.

Moving closer to the stricken Naomi, he lowered himself slowly to the floor, but was suddenly distracted by a shadow looming to his left. It was the last thing he remembered as a crashing blow from a heavy wooden pole hit him full in the face; he stumbled but did not fall until the second blow landed on the back of his head and he fell face down.

Charles took off his safari coat and covered Naomi as she tried to raise herself from the floor. He looked fondly at her and whispered, "Enough is enough! This must not happen again."

The fat man lay still for some minutes but then staggered to his feet just in time to see the old, battered taxi drive away in a cloud of dust.

41

SIX DAYS TO GO, MAY 1982

The normal Monday morning in Kitwe is mundane. The weekend of play is over, the shops are empty and mineworkers walking to work do so with sullen faces, not looking forward to the week ahead.

Things were different on this particular Monday morning in May. It was carnival week, and colourful flowers, banners and posters were being mounted in every available position, each wishing a joyous time for all. The larger banners that hung from buildings promoted the agricultural show starting on Thursday through to Saturday evening; the last event would be staged in the main arena.

Most of the banners were bright and colourful, each sponsored by a main supplier, the biggest being Coca-Cola. It was the start of an exciting week. The foyer of the Edinburgh Hotel was busy, and the box office positioned inside was attending to a long queue of people waiting to purchase standing-only tickets.

Martin took a couple of days' holiday from work, to ensure that arrangements were carried out smoothly and to plan. There was one important thing that worried him: the availability of the boxing ring.

He had agreed to use the same ring that he had used at the dinner show two years previously, but remembered it was very large and immensely heavy. He thought it should be much easier this time; installation would be in the open air with plenty of room for access, unlike the Edinburgh Hotel.

He walked into the foyer to check the initial sales and to ensure the funds were being controlled and the money bagged correctly. After all, this was Africa and money could disappear quickly; it was important that it was banked as soon as possible after bagging. His two trusty cashiers, he felt, were capable of handling the situation and responsible enough to check regularly that the numbers of tickets sold matched the takings.

One of them, Eddie, called out. "Martin, I have received passes for the cocktail party on Friday – you know, the party before your show – and would appreciate it if you took them before I give them away," he joked.

"How many?" asked Martin.

"Six, but I am sure the council will send more if you ask them!"

Martin picked up the tickets, made his way to his car and drove back to work. He used the company facsimile for messaging; he needed to clear up some contractual issues with the visiting personnel and to advise them of some changes to their itineraries. The messages were positive and confirmed the time of arrival; Martin phoned the taxi company and confirmed pick-up times.

Everything was coming together nicely and tickets were being sold at such a terrific rate, he decided to pay a visit to the TV studios and check if the outside broadcasting team would be available for the show.

Although his golf friends were not particularly interested in boxing it would be a nice gesture if he supplied them with complimentary tickets for the cocktail party and the main show. Charles may not want to come due to the exposure; he would have to make that decision for himself. Wolfgang would use his own allocation of tickets at his discretion, probably for business clients.

On Thursday he received a call from the TV producer. "Hi, Martin, Sol here. I understand that you were trying to contact me regarding live TV coverage of the two main events on Saturday?"

"Yes, that's right – is it a possibility?" asked Martin.

"Yes, we can normally set that up on the outside broadcast facility, but unfortunately we only have one vehicle and President Kaunda requires it for some party political broadcast on Saturday afternoon, and that will be for the rest of the day. However, what we can do is record some footage, then show it during the sports slot the day after."

There was a pause as Martin tried to hide his annoyance. "OK, it is what it is, Sol. It will be great to replay on Sunday, especially if it is favourable for our boys."

"OK, leave it with me. See you later."

Martin paused by the telephone, and before he had time to think about it further the phone rang again.

"Hello, Valeron here."

"Good afternoon, Martin; George Webster."

"George, nice to hear from you." It wasn't, and he grimaced.

"I read in the *Boxing News* all about your show on Saturday; don't normally read that paper, but read it at the barber's shop, would you believe?"

"Unusual," replied Martin.

"Just a quick call with reference to our man Coughlin – any news about him down there?"

"No... er, no!" replied Martin.

"I reckon that he is in Southern Africa somewhere; this comes from our international surveillance team who monitor calls around the world. It seems that our man has been busy contacting his bank in Jersey; we know he is in the southern hemisphere on the African continent."

"Well, that could be absolutely anywhere within three thousand miles."

"Yes, I am aware of that, but we are closing the gap. Although he is slowly becoming a second priority, he is still part of my portfolio and I want to clear the matter up."

"I understand that, George, and will as usual let you know if he surfaces."

"Thanks, Martin; speak with you soon." George put the phone down.

The pre-show cocktail party was scheduled to start at six in the evening. It was a cool time of day and allowed the invitees to mingle without the sun burning them. Cocktail mixers were difficult to come by in Zambia, so Martin purchased a moderate amount and had them flown in by Zambian Airways especially for the evening.

The party was an outside promotion; the idea was to capture the romanticism of a starlit African evening, so the covers and stalls were set up on open ground.

The show was initially set up to provide businesses with the chance to promote their products and merchandise, and local retailers to sell produce from stalls. The retailers set up in a pattern of three avenues, each connected to allow the party attendees to stroll around without going back on themselves. There was an area between the avenues that acted as a muster area, a place where people could assemble and just talk amongst themselves. The vendors sold everything from African carvings to electronics, and the bars were set up appropriately to ensure the attendees had drinks.

Martin agreed to meet Brendan at one of the gathering spaces, where they could drink a beer and greet the visitors as they mingled. Each of them had a network of friends and acquaintances, and made full use of these as they talked and joked with them. They continued socialising with the people filtering through the avenues, but soon gravitated towards each other to have a natter and reflect on the local gossip.

A sports commentator called Dennis Loewe soon interrupted them; he was his usual self and talked incessantly. His voice was so loud Martin wondered why he used a microphone during broadcasts. The introductions were carried out quickly; Martin recognised Loewe but not the lady so as they made eye contact he stuck out his hand to Dennis and made his own introduction, then he introduced Brendan.

Dennis then did his part. "Please can I introduce Aileen? She is a visitor to Kitwe and asked me if I could show her around and introduce her to a few people," explained Dennis.

"Are you here for the agricultural show, or is it just a coincidence that you are here tonight?" Brendan asked, as he was obviously attracted to her.

"I am in Lusaka on official business, but whilst I am in Zambia I decided to travel here to do a favour for a friend," she explained.

"That is very kind of you to think of your friend, especially when it requires such a detour, but we are happy that you did and we enjoy your company." Brendan was being extremely courteous.

Martin interjected, "So your friend is female and from Zimbabwe?" He was trying to be social and show an interest in Aileen's travels.

"No, no, she is actually Zambian but lives with her boyfriend in the Transkei."

"The Transkei?" Brendan was inquisitive.

"Yes, it is called 'the homelands'; a country within a country set up by the Afrikaners to house the indigenous people of South Africa – I mean the black people of South Africa."

"What is the capital?" asked Martin.

"Umtata."

"That's interesting."

Aileen went on. "Actually, her boyfriend is Ghanaian; he is an English teacher and wants to move back to Ghana, but she does not possess a passport at present, so I am here to help her get one."

"Do you work for a consulate or something?" Brendan asked.

She laughed. "No, I work for Amnesty International, but can pull a few strings, I hope."

"That is very considerate of you, Aileen. I am impressed."

Aileen smiled proudly.

"This woman's boyfriend, Aileen – what is his name?" Martin asked.

"His name? Oh, it is Dr Kwasi Nzema – you may have met him as he did live and work here in Kitwe."

Brendan was never normally lost for words, but in this instance both he and Martin were struck dumb.

"Is there something wrong? Did you know him?" asked Aileen.

"No – er, no," said Brendan. "I have heard of him, but did not know him. Nevertheless, he is in good hands, and I hope that you can get what you are here for."

42

A TIME TO REJOICE!

Dennis Loewe was fidgety, and was soon bored with the discussion. "Anyway, my friends, we must move on; there are some people I need to see before they leave so I must get busy. It has been a pleasure."

"By the way, Dennis, before you go, can I extend an invitation to you and Aileen for the boxing show tomorrow night?"

"Well, I am travelling back to Lusaka tomorrow morning, but perhaps Aileen would like to go?"

"Would you? We would look after you," laughed Martin.

"I would be delighted – although I am here alone, does that matter?" She went on, "It would be great to go to an international boxing event; it is something new, and I will look forward to it."

"Where are you staying?" Martin asked.

"With friends at the German Embassy; they have guest suites."

"Then I will have a car pick you up tomorrow, and don't worry about company – you will sit at the ringside with someone very interesting. You will like her."

"Thank you, Martin, and I bid you all goodnight."

The two friends waited until they were out of earshot, and watched Aileen disappear from view.

"What was that all about?" Brendan was beside himself.

"What the hell do we do, Brendan? We need a home contact for her, wherever she lives."

"Do you think it best to tell Naomi now, or perhaps it will be another disappointment if things do not work out?"

"Look, I will take the tickets down to the embassy early tomorrow with a bunch of flowers and advise Aileen that someone will pick her up at, say, ten o'clock in the morning, entertain her for most of the day and then drop and pick her up for the evening show. Unfortunately I will be busy all day Saturday so it will be impossible for me to do that, but I would certainly appreciate any help."

Brendan shook his head. "I need to go to the foundry in the morning."

"It seems that Charles is the only one of us who may be available; I hope he can do it."

"But he should be primed beforehand," urged Brendan.

Martin picked up his phone; it rang six times, and he became agitated, but a few seconds later the phone was answered.

"Hi, Charles; Martin here. Is Naomi with you?"

"No, she is visiting the Ghanaian community – why?"

Martin explained the situation and told his friend that it was pure coincidence, discovering Aileen. "It looks like we have located Kwasi at last, and perhaps the children are with him?"

"Yes, of course I will help; I am so bloody excited, I want to go and see this woman right now." Charles seemed to be climbing down the telephone.

"Keep calm now, and especially in the morning when you pick her up. Be at your best, and try if you can to have an intelligent conversation without getting her excited. If you do she may depart without giving us the information we need."

"Thanks for the lecture, but I am Irish so I know all about turning on the charm; something you English know nothing about."

"Thank you for that, but just remember that you are a fugitive so please do not get in the spotlight, or you may regret it."

"Oh, and by the way, do not say anything to Naomi; not yet anyway. We do not want further disappointment."

A CAUTIOUS TIME

Charles was excited, and it was difficult to suppress this when he met Naomi at his home later in the evening.

"I will be busy helping Martin tomorrow, my dear, and will not see you until late evening."

"That's fine, Charles; I intend to spend the day with Pet. She is leaving Zambia for a new life in England soon, so it will be nice to spend time with her before she goes."

"Why don't you let me pick you up at, say, six and you and Pet can come to the show? If she doesn't want to come there is a lady from the homelands who is here by herself; she wants company."

"I will look forward to that."

"OK, that's fine. Let's have our meal outside; the sky is clear, the stars are shining and at the moment, all is well."

He thought that she would certainly think the stars were shining brightly if she knew what was arranged for the next day.

43

THE SHOW,
MAY 1982

It was seven o'clock in the morning and the sun was hot, with not a cloud in the sky to temper the heat. It was going to be a long day.

Charles was up early. He shaved and showered and selected a short-sleeved striped shirt with a button-down collar. He matched this with a pair of light grey slacks and black loafers. His hair was a mess after the shower so he carefully used the hairdryer and then applied gel.

Looking in the mirror, he looked presentable and ready for the day ahead, even if he was three hours ahead of schedule.

Martin checked that all the participating boxers were primed and ready before he reviewed the timeline for the day; Wolfgang had prepared their breakfasts; and all were currently going through their exercise routines.

They would then take a long brisk walk and Wolfgang would check their weights at regular intervals.

He then went to the showground and checked that the ring was installed correctly, the ropes bound neatly, and all safety measures adhered to. After his experience of his first promotion in Zambia it was important to check that all the sponsors' advertising boards were in the correct position and words spelt correctly.

He anticipated that some fans would want to get to their seats up to two hours before the start of the event, it would save them queuing for drinks and snacks later when the stadium was full. The ticket collectors and stewards would need to be ready also two hours before the show was scheduled to start.

Early in the afternoon he dropped in at the lodge where the boxers were staying to ensure that they were taking a nap. He then went back home to change into something suitable for the heat. He chose a lightweight blue jacket with long dark blue trousers, and to finish he added a colourful bow tie to complement his shirt.

CHARLES'S DILEMMA

At exactly ten o'clock, Charles – looking especially dapper; his left hand clutching a beautiful array of roses, his right holding car keys, tickets and a name tag – entered the German Embassy. It was a house with about fourteen rooms on the first floor and half that amount on the ground floor. The building was an annex to the main embassy in Lusaka, and used to assist expatriate mineworkers.

"Ms Aileen, please." He addressed the African clerk at the desk.

"Does she expect you, sir? She is a guest staying in the annex; I will find out. Please wait here."

The clerk disappeared through some very high doors behind him.

Charles suddenly had doubts. Would she be in? Had she felt intimidated by Martin and Brendan's questions last night? He only hoped that she was still here and coming to the show.

He waited for fifteen minutes and stopped pacing to sit on one of the luxury chairs positioned around the room. After some time he checked his watch again; it was now thirty minutes.

Just then the clerk returned. He wore a very sober expression as he approached Charles.

"Yes?" Charles asked."

"She is coming, sir, and apologises for her delay." The clerk nodded and returned to his desk.

After another fifteen minutes Aileen glided through the door, looking quite radiant in a flowing multi-coloured dress. Charles found her very attractive – her light brown skin suggested she had a mixed-race background, but this, he felt, enhanced her beauty. Her hair was straight and held high, with a suggestion of a small ponytail; wisps of hair were expertly clipped to hang graciously on her forehead. He wondered what exactly she did for Amnesty International.

"It's Charles, isn't it?" She smiled as she held out her hand.

"It is, my dear, and these are for you." He handed her the flowers.

"They are beautiful, let me put them in water." She handed them to the clerk. "Where are we going so early?" She smiled.

"Have you taken breakfast?"

"Yes, but I eat little."

He gestured with his hand to the car. She walked beside him and looked over to him.

"Have we met before?" she asked.

"No, ma'am, I don't think so."

"It's just, I feel I know your face from somewhere."

Charles changed the subject; he was alarmed at her question. "If you have no objection we will drive around Kitwe and I will show you the places of interest. Then we'll stop for morning tea at the lodge and, if we have time, take a short drive to a small hotel just outside of town and have lunch."

"That sounds most entertaining." Aileen seemed matter-of-fact.

"It will give you a couple of hours to freshen up afterwards before I pick you up for the show."

"Sounds good."

They started their drive and Charles, trying to be tactful, started his enquiry. "What do you do for Amnesty International?" he asked.

"I am personal secretary to the assistant to the director general."

"Does that require travel as part of your remit?" he asked.

"Occasionally I travel with my boss, and sometimes I volunteer for tasks that may require travelling, but I can only do so when he is not around."

"And is that what you are doing now: travelling and helping out?"

"Yes, I suppose so."

He did not want to pressure her with too many questions; nor did he know how to approach the question of children.

Before he could think of another tack, she began her own enquiry. "What do you do here, Charles? Do you work for the mines?"

"No, I am here to assist Martin and his partner Wolfgang with the promotions."

"Is that full-time?"

"No, but I am a mechanic so I do some casual work around the town too, but mainly I help Martin and Wolfgang."

"Do you like it here? Have you travelled?" she asked inquisitively.

"Well, I am Irish and have hiked around Europe and England, so I thought Africa would be interesting. It is." He lied, but wanted to get back to his queries without recourse.

They finally stopped for tea and exchanged general queries, but it soon began to feel like an inquest. At two o'clock he dropped her back at the embassy and said he would call for her at four o'clock. He was disappointed with his efforts and, unable to speak with Martin, instead phoned Brendan.

"OK, Charles, you pick her up and I suggest Naomi sit with her at the ringside; she will have a more feminine approach. I will drive down to inform Martin, and you ask Naomi to cancel her date with Petula as we do not have a ringside seat for her."

Brendan was lucky to catch Martin at home; he was just leaving the house when the phone rang.

"Hi, Martin; Brendan here. This is the plan…"

44

THE PLAN

Naomi was not amused when Brendan and Jim informed her of the change in plan. She had expected a day's shopping with her friend and now Pet was ill and Brendan had redirected her to the ringside to sit with a woman she had never met! She was not happy.

Charles accompanied Aileen to her seat at about 5.30; she was shortly joined by Naomi, and both ladies were dressed nicely but suitably for the event, in trousers and loose cotton tops. It did not take long before they were chatting happily and sharing their experiences.

It was after the first fight that Naomi mentioned that she was separated from her children, and that, although she called herself Naomi Zimba, her married name was Nzema.

Aileen seemed confused, and turned to speak with Naomi. "This is either a total coincidence or a bizarre situation, but I am currently pursuing a passport for a lady who approached me for help, as she plans to marry a man by the name of Nzema."

"Is that man by himself or does he have children with him?" Naomi had lost her joviality and looked seriously at her companion.

"He has three children, I think, but I may be guessing as I have not met him yet," advised Aileen.

Naomi head tilted her back straight she became rigid with excitement, but if she was wrong she must play the situation down until she found out the whole story.

Aileen took up the conversation before Naomi could express herself. "Naomi, please may I change the subject and ask you something before I forget? It concerns your friend Charles Siddons. Mr Siddons shared a lovely day with me today, he was the perfect gentleman, but I feel that we have met previously."

Naomi was acutely aware of Charles's dilemma, and tried to change the subject.

"But I am sure that I have met Mr Siddons before; if not face to face, certainly his name is familiar.

"When did you first meet him?"

"Oh, he is a friend of Brendan; they have known him for some time, possibly since he arrived from Ireland."

The second fight had been announced and the bell rang for the first round. There was a lot of noise in the arena, and because of this the women ceased to chat during rounds, but made up for this between rounds during the one-minute break.

"Let us go to the back, perhaps find a seat at the outside restaurant and have a drink. We will find it more suitable for a normal discussion without shouting at each other." Aileen suggested.

"OK. That sounds fine."

"You have a strong Afrikaans accent – are you from South Africa?"

"Well, yes, I am originally. My folks are from Lundazi in Zambia but they actually married in Johannesburg, and that's where my accent comes from, but then I was educated in Swaziland and speak German as well." Naomi smiled.

"A private school?"

"Yes, I was lucky; it was paid for by my grandfather. He was a white farmer, you understand?"

"I, er, think so, but that does not matter; you had the opportunity."

"But, Aileen, seriously, I want you to be honest with me. I am a mother who was forcibly separated from her children;

225

it happened and I cannot explain to you what that does to a mother, not having her children around her."

Her face grew sullen, her lips curled downwards, and she bowed her head and wept. She was ashamed of her weakness; it felt disrespectful to her companion.

"Naomi, I am sorry – and you think that this lady is the person who has your children?"

"It is not the woman; she is just another in the life of Kwasi. It is the children. If only he told me that they are safe; I do not know if they are well or in poor health, lost or whatever, and now what you say suggests to me that they are not only safe, but with him – and so close! All I want to do is see them and tell them I love them and miss them. I must see them. Excuse me please, Aileen, let us walk; people are looking."

They stood up and strolled around the perimeter of the arena. The noise was once again deafening; it seemed the main fight was on.

Naomi forced a smile and looked at Aileen. "It must be Musankabala; he is the favourite and I know from discussions with my friends that he is the best. If he wins this fight he should fight for a world title or something."

Naomi fell silent as the cheers echoed around the arena. A single voice would be lost. The noise continued, building to one huge cheer followed by a loud murmur. Naomi and Aileen turned away from the arena and walked back into the avenues of market stalls. The traders were giving away gifts, this being the last day of the event.

One stallholder shouted across to his friend on a stall opposite, who was trying to give away some trinkets to a group of children. "Who won the fight?"

Before the friend could answer, one of the young girls snapped, "Musankabala, by knockout."

The vendor shrugged his shoulders.

"Naomi, I do not know what to say. I have not seen the children or Kwasi, but I know that he is teaching at a university in Umtata. I cannot divulge his address to you, you know I must have loyalties, but I also have sympathy for you, and I understand what you are going through."

"Get your passport, do what you have to do, but you need to tell me where my children are. I implore you!" Naomi was in tears. She stopped walking and Aileen took the opportunity to look deeply into her eyes.

"I have told you that Kwasi is close and the children are safe but you must promise me that you will do nothing for a week and will allow me to do what I came here to do. I assure you that Kwasi is going nowhere for now, and I will not mention that I have met you."

"I promise, then, that I will not contact him for a week, and when I do I will not mention your name."

"Good luck, Naomi, you deserve it, and I hope that you are reunited with your children."

Naomi nodded.

"I must go now, finish my business here and return before my director gets back next Monday, so I will bid you goodbye and try and find Charles to drive me back to the embassy. He did tell me where to find him."

"Goodbye, Aileen, and thank you."

After Aileen had gone, Naomi wanted to speak with Charles, but he would be home later after taking Aileen home. She walked from the stadium to the bus terminal; it was a long walk and took her an hour and twenty minutes.

She found the ticket office and approached the clerk. "I want to go from here to Umtata in the Transkei next week. Please advise me on how I can do this, and the cost of the travel."

"That is a long way, ma'am, a long way; it will take you many hours."

"Yes, I know, but please tell me. It is important."

The clerk looked at some papers and shook his head. "Ma'am, it will take you two days and you must travel to Lusaka, then on to Johannesburg and then the Transkei. It may be many, many buses."

"How much will it cost?"

"Plenty."

"How much is plenty?"

"Ma'am, it will be about four hundred kwacha."

"Thank you."

She hailed a taxi; it was a white transit van with seats fitted in the back. Only one seat was vacant, so she sat and later the taxi dropped her at the institute, from where she walked back to her house.

She waited for Charles to phone her.

TELEPHONE CALL TO LONDON, MONDAY MORNING

"Is this the right number for the Foreign Intelligence Offices?"

"Yes, ma'am, which extension, please?"

"My name is Aileen Santos; I work for the Amnesty International."

"Yes, ma'am, but please give me the extension you want."

"You will need to tell me that after I explain the situation."

"OK, then please proceed."

"I saw a photograph on the board in my office: an Irish fugitive called Barney Coughlin. He was wanted for questioning by your organisation."

"One moment, ma'am." He checked some papers on his desk. "Putting you through."

"Webster here, can I help?"

"Mr Webster, my name is Aileen Santos, I live in the Transkei in South Africa. I know where a Mr Barney Coughlin is living and I understand you want him for questioning."

"Er, yes we do – can you please advise me of your details and the information you know about Coughlin?"

"Yes, I will tell you what I know. But one thing: please do not send further enquiries to me by mail; I need to confirm my position over this situation with my superior first. Is that clear, Mr Webster?"

"That's absolutely fine with me, and should I have further questions we will speak again by phone."

"Thank you. This is all I know..." She went on to explain what had happened over the past two days.

George Webster was now suspicious that his old confidant Martin Valeron was not telling him the whole truth. Was it a coincidence that he and Coughlin (alias Charles Siddons) now knew each other in Africa, or had they actually colluded when they were at Sullom Voe?

Webster gave the situation some thought, and decided to confirm his action with his director. But first he would make a call. Without wasting another minute he rang the British Embassy in Lusaka, explained the situation and advised them that an order for Coughlin's arrest would be sent in the next day.

At four in the afternoon he entered the director's office.

"Good afternoon, sir; can I update you quickly on Coughlin, our IRA fugitive?"

"Go ahead, Webster." The director was curt.

"We have located him in Kitwe, Zambia, and can bring him in for questioning today if necessary. Do you advise this?"

"Why not, but I suggest that we get an extradition order set up, and in the meantime have the local police take him in for questioning. Once the extradition is arranged you can pay a visit to clarify what we will do with him once we have him deported back here."

There was a pause before the director went on. "I was thinking that in the first instance this might not be worth it, but in view of Mrs Siddons' recent claim we have no alternative."

"OK, sir, we will bring him in and, arrange the extradition; I will go down there and question him before flying him back here."

"That's it."

"Thank you, sir."

"Shut the door behind you, Webster, that's a good chap."

45

AN IMMINENT ARREST

The police station in Kitwe seemed overcrowded at the best of times, and was made worse by the large waistlines of the officers who squeezed past each along the corridors, or in the office at tea breaks. The situation got even worse if the dartboard was in use.

Now things were going to get a whole lot worse. It was Wednesday 2nd June 1982, and the commanding officer in Kitwe had received a message from the high commission in Lusaka.

Geoffrey Banda stared at the facsimile. The message was instructing him to arrest a foreign citizen residing in Kitwe. He was to send two of his officers to Ndola, where a further two from the local force would join them. The men should be firearms experts and intelligent enough to show restraint and compromise should the situation arise. This was serious, he thought; an international interaction. Who were his most reliable team members?

Banda walked quickly from his office and made an announcement. "Stop everything you are doing and take a seat at your desks. I have an announcement to make."

The whole office was suddenly in turmoil as the officers all headed for their own desks, bumping into each other and knocking chairs onto the floor. It was pandemonium until everyone was settled and awaiting the brief from the boss.

The chief cleared his throat and stood glaring at his team, ready to give his orders. He looked bewildered, and thrust his hands into his pockets, trying to locate the fax.

"Felix, the fax is in my office; hurry, bring it to me."

The unfortunate man hurried to Banda's office and, after a few minutes, returned with a crumpled piece of paper.

"I have received an important instruction from the high commission in Lusaka. We are to locate and arrest a man wanted for questioning regarding a number of offences that have occurred in the United Kingdom. The man should be treated as dangerous and all precautions taken by those who are involved in his arrest.

"I will nominate two officers who will join forces with two others from the Ndola force. The two nominations from here will be Officer Bishonga and Officer Makobi; please make yourselves ready to travel as soon as possible. The rest of you are on alert; as soon as the man is in transit we need to be ready to receive him. He will be held here until an MI6 agent arrives from London."

Approximately three hours later, four officers armed with rifles and old British Army pistols were on their way to the house where the alleged offender was living. They pulled up in a cloud of dust and moved swiftly into position around the house. The senior officer strode up to the door and knocked hard.

In just a few minutes a tall, pretty local lady opened the door. "Yes, what can I do for you?" Her heavy, guttural accent was pronounced.

"Good afternoon, ma'am; I am looking for a man by the name of Charles Siddons. He may also go under the name of Barney Coughlin."

"What do you want from him?" she barked. "We are very busy at the moment, so state what you want with him."

232

Charles had overheard what was going on, and joined Naomi at the door. "Yes, Officer, I am Charles Siddons; how can I help?"

"I am here to arrest you and take you back to Kitwe Police Station. I have the house surrounded, so I would appreciate it if you came without any further ado. I will need to handcuff you, and also advise you that anything you say may be used in evidence against you in a court of law."

"What, here in Zambia or…?"

"The British government has applied for extradition, but you will be held here until this order has been authorised."

Charles smiled. "Nonsense, man; please come in, all of you."

The four officers shuffled into the living room. Their rifles were carried clumsily, as if they were not used to them.

"Put those things down, and Naomi will make you a cup of tea."

"That is not necessary; we must be on our way."

"Yes, yes, Officer, but you must realise that all this fuss is unnecessary; it's all a misunderstanding."

"What do you mean, a misunderstanding, sir?"

"Well, last week I was asked by the high commission to bring my passport into the station, but due to our agricultural show, I totally forgot. Obviously there has been some misunderstanding and the high commission has overreacted."

Naomi entered the room and handed out tea and biscuits to the four policemen.

"Now, what I suggest is that you return to the station with my passport and inform the high commission of this, and I will pick it up on Friday when this has been cleared up."

"Those are not our orders, sir; you will need to come with us now."

"You four will look absolutely stupid, especially when I tell the papers that, after all the support we have given to the police

233

benevolent fund, you have treated me in this way." Charles added, "You know that I was in partnership with Lemmie Chipili? Now, what I will do is add to our donation by providing expenses for you and your team, given your undue troubles, and allow you to return to your stations."

"That is very considerate, sir, but I have my orders."

"Take this and go, and if your senior is not satisfied then you can return here and collect me, and you can keep the expenses."

Charles handed out the notes. The officers were at first reluctant, but a month's pay for an hour's work sounded too good to be true, and they stuffed the notes into their pockets.

"OK, Officers, thank you for coming and I will see you all on Friday when I come to the station to collect my passport."

After he closed the door he turned to Naomi, who was collecting up the dirty cups and saucers. "Do not say anything, but listen; pack the things you need for a two-week stay. You are going to Umtata tonight, I will book a taxi now."

"But how will I get there, Charles?"

"I have collected some funds from the guys at work and we have enough for you to get there and back, plus you can stay for a week if you want to."

"But it will take so long, Charles."

"You will fly via Johannesburg to Umtata, stay in the local hotel for up to a week and return the same way."

"But what will you do, Charles? They will be back, and with a much bigger force; you will not be able to bluff them a second time."

"Never mind me, I am used to it and will let you know where I am." He looked at his lovely friend."

"Don't worry, I will be OK; just you go and find your kids. They are more important."

They held each other tightly for a few moments, before he pushed her out of the door and into a waiting taxi.

Charles caught her just before the driver pulled away. "Just remember, Naomi: you are doing everything right. Then make sure that everything you do, you do with your head held high!"

He stood back as the driver accelerated away.

46

UMTATA

The long wait at Jan Smuts Airport in Johannesburg made Naomi very tired, and she had hardly completed half the journey. Not even the excitement of potentially seeing her children after such a long time raised her spirits.

The flight to Umtata was short and she avoided taking on a conversation with the man sitting next to her, and the more he spoke to her the more irritable she became. The time it took for the plane to circle whilst waiting to land seemed an eternity for Naomi, and once it had touched down she was ecstatic. Her excitement was beyond belief, and she almost fainted.

She was landing in an area that was a young country but extremely important in terms of African history. The area was nominated as the black homelands, and in 1976 the Transkei was granted independence but not recognised outside of South Africa. The town called Mthatha served as the capital and later became known as Umtata, and a new airport was currently being built, though the original runway continued to be in service. The area was especially historic as both President Nelson Mandela and his famous colleague Walter Sisulu originated from there.

The luggage turntable whirled around, empty; the ground staff were having trouble delivering the cases, and the passengers waited patiently. It gave Naomi the opportunity to think of her strategy; how she would approach the principal and Kwasi when the time came. Her biggest challenge would be the children, and how she would stop herself from breaking down when she finally met them again after such a long time.

The man who had sat next to her on the plane sidled up to her and again tried to start a conversation, but she had seen this all before and wanted no part of his hospitality.

"Ma'am, I have my car parked just outside the airport and it would be my honour to take you to town." He smiled; he seemed a little creepy, she thought.

"No, thank you. It is so nice of you to offer me your services, but I have someone who will pick me up," she lied.

A few moments later her case was hurled towards her, and in an instant she had it in her hands and was making for the taxi rank.

"The university, please." Naomi had made her mind up quickly.

"Yes, ma'am, I will drop you at the reception, but it will take some time due to traffic."

"Do not worry; just get me there before the reception closes." She checked her watch; it was five minutes past three in the afternoon.

At precisely three minutes to four o'clock she strode into the principal's secretary's office. She was sitting at her desk chatting with another lady – perhaps the typist, Naomi thought – and they ignored her.

"The principal, please," Naomi said with authority.

The secretary looked up, agitated at being disturbed. "Er, Mr Sisoko is in conference and not available until tomorrow."

"OK, so please book me in for then. My name is Zimba, Naomi Zimba, I am the estranged wife of Kwasi Nzema and please show me where I shall meet with him tomorrow?"

"I will book you in to see him at 9.30, and his office is the one behind you." The secretary looked down and noted the details. "What is the matter you wish to discuss with him?"

"I will tell you after I see him." But instead of leaving the premises, Naomi walked directly to the principal's office door and entered. The secretary scrambled towards her, not expecting her to enter the office without permission.

"Ma'am, please – you can see I am busy and I have to complete this report tonight, so please make an appointment with me tomorrow."

"Sir, we have not met before but the reason I have come to see you will not wait a minute longer."

Before he could protest further she was in full flow, and the principal, though clearly annoyed, nevertheless listened.

"My children were taken from me illegally by my husband Dr Kwasi Nzema some years ago, and now I have information that he teaches here at the university. I need to see them now, and will not wait another moment."

"Mrs Nzema please, it is not under my jurisdiction to tell you who works here or what their private life entails." He intended to scold her further, but she stopped him in his tracks.

"Sir, I once again inform you that a teacher working at this university has three children in his care, but has done this illegally, and what is more, he intends to get married to another woman in a few weeks and commit bigamy. If you do not address this situation immediately I will go to the press and concoct a story they will love to publish, especially with your name in the headlines."

"That's preposterous." He glanced at his secretary standing at the open door. "Sandra, please get Nzema up here and sort this out."

The secretary's attitude seemed to have changed. A group of women from the office had joined her, and they were agitated and made no secret of the fact regarding the children.

"Come, ladies, please clear the office; we will get this situation clarified very quickly."

The principal turned to Naomi. "Please, Mrs Nzema, wait in my office and we will resolve this as quickly as possible." He sighed, and thought to himself that he could have done without this unfortunate situation.

47

NDOLA

There was uproar at the police station in Kitwe. Superintendent Banda was shouting at his officers seated in front of him.

"When I give an order, it must be obeyed. We are under the control of the high commission, and after today they will probably fire me and all of you simultaneously. Now please move quickly; I want two cars and eight officers to return to Ndola without further delay. I expect this dangerous fugitive to be under lock and key by tonight, so please do not fail me. Arrest him by force if necessary, then shackle him, and I want him in our cells before any of you go home. Do you all understand? Because if you don't, then do not bother to come to work tomorrow. Now, let us have action."

The house in Ndola where Charles had lived was now under siege. The eight officers had surrounded the house and their lead man, Mwale, was waiting for a reply to his heavy banging on the door. But there was nothing. Mwale instructed his men to be ready to enter the property by force.

After a few minutes the door was broken down and four armed men entered. There was no sound or movement, and they moved through the house as quickly as possible, checking for any sign of life.

There was nothing.

UMTATA

When Kwasi reached the secretary's office he had to walk through two lines of university staff. They were waiting for him to arrive, and made his entry uncomfortable by hissing at his every move, showing resentment for the treatment he had given his wife. He was a tall, thin man and towered above them all, and had to bow his head when he entered Sisoko's office, but stopped abruptly when he saw Naomi sitting cross-legged on a chair next to Sisoko's desk.

"Have you brought me trouble, Naomi?"

"No more than you have given me these past years. Have you the children?" she asked.

Kwasi ignored her and sat at the opposite side of the desk. She was controlling her every emotion, but his silence infuriated her more.

The next forty-five minutes of discussion revolved around various events in their marriage, but the inevitable question regarding the children: had Kwasi taken them away from their mother illegally?

After listening for a while to the dialogue, the principal held his hand up. He had heard enough, and now wanted to go home. "OK, OK, I have the one and only solution to resolve this issue immediately, and I will tell you what is going to be done in a few days when I have had more time to think about it.

"In the meantime, Kwasi, you will need to advise me of your intentions regarding your wife in the long term. In the short term you will ensure that your wife has accommodation and food whilst she is here, but most of all that she has access to the children. Do you understand?"

"Yes, sir."

"May I suggest that she visits them tomorrow at your house, and every day until we get this situation sorted out? The

241

provisional details will need to be discussed later, when we make a decision as to whether this needs to be settled by the courts, or whether an agreement between the two of you can be made now.

"OK, then it is time we all went home. I have decided to advise the governors of what has transpired here today, but I hope that we can resolve this without it going to them on a formal basis."

THE ULTIMATE REUNION

The next day a car picked Naomi up and drove her slowly through the streets of Umtata. With each turn she expected the residential area to come into view, but it was over forty minutes later that the car edged through the gates of the university halls, took a left towards the staff accommodation and parked in a small car park.

The driver switched off the engine and, without looking at Naomi in the back seat, explained, "Mr Nzema's house is 55A; it is the fifth house in the road opposite us." He pointed to a corner.

Naomi exited the car and walked in that direction. She had the feeling that, through all the windows along the road, people were looking out at her. She remembered that Charles had told her to keep her head high whatever the situation, and, feeling conspicuous and alone, she forced her neck and back to straighten and walked with purpose.

Quite unexpectedly, she heard a cry. "Mama, Mama – over here!"

She looked, and standing in the doorway of a house on her left were three children. A maid was holding them back, but in a second two of them broke free and ran towards their mother.

The smallest of the three held back, as if unsure of what to expect. They met, it seemed, running too fast, as they crashed into their mother and hugged her. Naomi fell to her knees and encircled them with her arms.

The smallest child had decided to follow the other two and as he reached the trio Naomi pulled him in close to her.

She had never forgotten the anguish she had suffered when he had a heart operation some five years previously. She cried for joy; he looked so healthy.

They held this position for many minutes before Naomi could speak. The two oldest children, now twelve and eleven years old, remembered her and held her arms tightly.

"Children, my children, you have much to tell me. I want to know every detail, from the time that we were parted. We have time. And now you must open your presents." And they walked into the house where the maid had made breakfast.

The tallest and oldest child broke in. "We have three days off, just to see you."

His sister interrupted him; she did not want to be left out. "Mama we can stay with you in the hotel all of the time you are here."

"Well, that is a lovely thought, and I will enjoy these three days more than any I have ever had in my life." She was so happy.

After breakfast they walked back along the road to the car that had brought Naomi to her children. The driver smiled, and Naomi gave him instructions.

"Please drive, but take us somewhere close to where the birds sing the loudest."

48

SLIPPING HIS TAIL

The old Opel drove slowly through town. It passed Mulema Street, then took a turning into Alongo Road towards the centre of Ndola, the driver looking for a place to hide.

He noticed a discoloured white Toyota; it was parked adjacent to a plot of wasteland. Inside the cab were three rough looking individuals; through the open window they were talking with another man leaning on the offside door. As the driver passed the group he recognised the man on the outside, pulled to the side of the road, and quickly backed up in front of the white vehicle.

The three men in the white Toyota, on seeing a white stranger, moved swiftly to his vehicle and positioned themselves outside Charles's car door. It was a threatening gesture, and he tried to calm the situation before it escalated.

He held up his hand and slowly opened his window. "Hold up, brothers; that man leaning on your car is my friend George Mwanza." Charles pointed towards the man who had now moved under the shadow of a tree.

"What is you name?" one of the guys growled.

"Charles Siddons. He knows me well."

The man walked back to the tree and spoke with Mwanza and returned to Charles. "OK, man, George wants you to join him; savvy?"

"OK." Charles left his car and joined George.

"Well, if it is not my old friend Charles." Mwanza was grinning from ear to ear.

"Hi, George; it's great to see you, and by the way, thanks for the presents."

"The presents, man, what presents?" countered George.

"The python and leopard skins, but I had to ditch them; those skins are no longer legal in the UK."

"Look, man, that was just a taster; I still owe you but I will pay you back soon."

"George, please do not worry, you don't owe me a thing, but I need help, man. Your police force are out looking for me."

"Never – what is that all about? You killed somebody?"

"No, not quite; it's just an organisation that I was involved with some time ago, that's all."

"What organisation?"

"Forget it, George, it's in the past."

"Man have I underestimated you? Were you mixed up with Krays?"

"Look, forget about that – I must find a place to hide."

"Is that all? I can do that, man; come with me to the border near where we met, and if they get close just pop across to the DRC."

Charles did not say a word, but gazed at George.

"Give the car to the boys here; it will be out of your hands and they will not find you because of it, that's for sure."

"Do I stay with you?"

"Yes, we go now while you have the chance, but remember, I am not with you if they get close. It will be my life if they do, and do not ask me the reason."

"OK, George, I think I understand the situation let's go, and now I will owe you."

"That's for sure; you will owe me plenty, ha ha!"

49

JOURNEY TO AN UNKNOWN WORLD

That evening Charles spent the night in a very unkempt house in the township to the north of Kitwe.

Mwanza and his 'friends' slept in the two bedrooms and Charles on the settee with a coat to keep him warm. It was uncomfortable, and there was a lot of noise coming from a local bar.

Most of the night he tossed and turned, uncomfortable, his mind going over and over the plan for the next twelve hours. This time would be critical for his survival.

Mwanza had explained to his team that Charles would travel alone to Konkola by truck; where he would transfer from the mine truck to a small school bus. In the truck he would double up as a relief driver and on the bus he would act as an assistant teacher... The school bus would drop him at Mwanza's safe house, where he would stay until his new passport and air ticket were prepared. Mwanza and his colleagues would travel to the safe house in Konkola separately.

Charles was set to leave with the truck after the curfew lifted at six o'clock and should make the transfer at around twelve o'clock. It was agreed with Mwanza that should any of them be stopped and questioned, they would abide by the rule of silence.

Nothing was said between Charles and the other desperados whilst they waited in the house. Just before he left Mwanza wished Charles good luck and reminded him that he hoped to see him at the safe house." There were no goodbyes!

The journey was uneventful for the first hour. The road was clear, without roadblocks, and Charles was surprised that everything seemed normal.

However, things were to change, and as the truck approached the Chingola turn-off, four policemen were standing next to bamboo cane that stretched across one half of the road.

Large rocks obviously man-handled from the bush blocked the other half of the road.

The truck slowed and stopped adjacent to the first policeman. The other two armed officers kept off the road but were with rifles ready.

"Good day. May I see both of your identifications, please?" asked the policeman.

The driver handed over his ID card and driving licence.

"And yours." The officer looked over to Charles.

"My passport has been sent to the British Consulate for renewal, but I have my golf club membership card with me. It includes a photograph." Charles remained casual.

"It is not a legally binding document, I am afraid to tell you."

"I can take my passport into your station when I receive it," Charles lied. His original passport was held at Ndola Police Station and George was to supply him with a new one. He did not carry details of the document with him.

"I am afraid that is not permissible, sir. You must return with me to the main police station at Chingola, and we must obtain clearance from Lusaka Police Control." He paused and went on, "Foreigners to Zambia must have proof of identity with them at all times, so please, you must travel with me to Chingola now."

Charles stalled for a few seconds, and it gave him time to think. "Look, Officer, I am a working man and need to stay with this vehicle to help with the unloading at the yard in Konkola. Why can't we settle this thing now? Surely there must be a way?"

Another large truck had pulled up behind theirs, and the driver was becoming impatient, hooting his horn. The oncoming traffic on the other side of the road was also building up, and the officer in charge was becoming frustrated.

"Yes, please wait a moment until I finish talking to these truckers." He addressed Charles once more. "OK, I will need your address and movements over the next week." He paused and added, "You will need to report to our Konkola office within seven days, take your passport, and it is necessary to pay me two hundred dollars for the inconvenience."

"Officer, that sounds harsh, but I see that you are busy." Charles gave his personal details, which would be checked against his passport later, and handed over two hundred dollars to the officer.

The policeman nodded and waved them through, and, still counting his money, walked to the truck behind them. "Identification, please," he asked the driver.

Just before Charles was due to transfer to the school bus, the truck passed three police cars. They were attending to a road smash but moved to the side of the road and pulled in Charles and the truck.

"What can we do for you, Officer?"

"We need a lift to our station on the Chililabombwe road; are you going that way?"

"No, Officer, we will branch off towards Konkola, but one of you can sit in between us until then if you want?"

"Thank you, sir. Please proceed; we will try the next vehicle."

Charles was sweating as he arrived at the safe house, and he did not know whether it was the stress or the heat. He was glad when the houseboy showed him to a small room at the back of the house.

During his stay there Charles did not go outside, not even to brae or barbecue, and on the third day Mwanza visited. He walked into the house with a brown envelope and placed it slowly on the dining table next to Charles, who was making some notes.

"It is there, my friend; you owe me seven hundred American dollars and that is a special price, and includes flight and passport."

Charles gulped; he was in a predicament regarding his cash flow, which had now dried up. His access to the original Charles Siddons' account was now frozen, and any withdrawals would be traced. "Wait a moment, George; I need to check what cash I have on me."

Charles walked outside and with a hammer broke the heel of one of his shoes to see what was left of his cash. In one shoe he counted only five hundred dollars, and in the other he was relieved to count five thousand dollars.

He paid George and asked him when the ticket would be available.

"Be patient, my Irish friend; everything to him that waits."

He laughed and walked outside.

50

TWO WORLDS APART
JUNE 1983

On the 26th June 1980, Barney Coughlin, alias Charles Siddons, absconded from his job in the Shetlands and simultaneously terminated his alliance with the IRA. Now, three years later, he was on a flight from Lubumbashi International Airport to Addis Ababa. He sat in economy class at the rear of the plane and reflected on his time in Zambia.

His one regret was leaving its people. He thought of Naomi and hoped she was enjoying her time with her children; a rich reward for being so determined. He would have liked their association to continue, but his migration and the threat of imminent arrest made this impossible.

The times he had had in Zambia had been like a dream, and he was proud of his part in assisting Naomi in finding her children. It had been particularly special to see her face when she discovered where they were.

The situation as it turned out was an amazing coincidence; after all their hard work, the break had come with the unexpected arrival of Aileen at the trade fair. It had made Naomi the happiest person on the planet.

He would miss playing golf with his buddies, and hoped there would be no repercussions for Martin from his MI6 contact George Webster.

And the dubious George Mwanza – how important had that first meeting turned out to be? And how did he produce a replacement passport at short notice that included a photograph. Charles touched his new eyeglasses and quietly memorised his new name that George had so conveniently provided.

"Edward Copping," he said to himself.

George Mwanza had left 'Edward' at the departure gate. "Good luck, my man. Look after yourself." He pressed a piece of paper into his friend's hand and whispered, "Your contact in Ethiopia."

Edward scanned the paper; it contained a name and a telephone number. He read it again, then, before he could give his dubious friend a final hug and thank him, it was too late; George was already leaving the airport through the far exit doors. Edward squinted hard to see if anyone else was with him, and sure enough, he had his arms around the shoulders of two very shapely ladies.

When the flight was airborne and at cruising speed, Edward began to daydream. His mind turned to Mwanza; a mysterious person. Who was he? What did he do? He had helped Edward after he arrived in the country, and at the last minute had been there to save him. Deep down he felt that he did not want to know more; Mwanza might be his saviour, but his guardian angel he certainly wasn't.

The likeness of the passport photograph to Edward's own features was unbelievable, although the man in the photo had different eyeglasses and the shape of his face was rounder.

Edward had asked George, "What if this man has reported the passport lost?"

He replied, with a serious face, "He already has a new one, but if you don't like that one give it back. Too many questions my friend.

Edward Copping, alias Charles Siddons, alias Barney Coughlin, boarded the Ethiopian Airlines jet and took his seat for the capital. The flight was non-stop to Addis Ababa, and was scheduled to take four and a half hours.

He fell into a deep sleep, and his mind again played tricks on him. He dreamt that his contact in Ethiopia was George Webster!

He woke up, his forehead covered in sweat. A nightmare – how could he doubt George Mwanza?

UMTATA

Naomi had one day remaining of her stay with her three children. It had been a wonderful time and she had not laughed as much in her life as she had in these last few days.

She had discovered that, when she first arrived at the university, the secretary had overheard her story of Kwasi's deceit, and related this to the rest of the staff. They all made a point of demonstrating on behalf of Naomi to the principal and the governors, who immediately made sure that Kwasi supported Naomi with her every need. He was made to account for her expenses, access to the children, and the terms for her to see them in the future.

The flight back from Umtata to Lusaka via Johannesburg was bittersweet for Naomi. She had located her children, it was beyond belief after so long, and for that she thanked God.

Her next visit was planned for only a few months hence. The principal had offered her staff lodgings during her stay, and the school caretaker would be her driver. She felt honoured and privileged, and later wrote and thanked all those who had helped her to achieve this.

She became emotional, her thoughts taking her back to that wonderful Irishman, Charles. She hoped and prayed that he had escaped and was not now in a police cell. He did not deserve that. He was her best friend, and he had told her that, if caught, it may be years before he was released. Naomi had lost her man again.

The Lord gives and He takes, she thought.

ADDIS ABABA

Edward Copping walked from the departure gate at Addis Ababa Airport. He found a telephone kiosk, picked up the phone and dialled a number.

"Hello, this is Copping. Can I speak with Wekesa?"

"It is me; George told me to expect you." Wekesa's English was perfect.

"I have booked into the Ramada for three days; can you suggest something after that?" Edward was straight to the point.

"I am on your case Mr Copping and I have possibilities of work for you in Iraq, it will be working for a British company with interests there.

"Iraq? What type of work?" asked Edward.

"Building work."

"That sounds fine."

"OK, I will arrange your visa and job application. This will take a week, so you'd best extend your stay at the Ramada, and incidentally, this will cost you three thousand American dollars; is that OK?"

"Yes, that's fine."

The line buzzed, and the call was terminated.

EPILOGUE

A town can change its character quickly; one can revisit after only a few months and find it is not the same place as it was when one left.

Times change and local councils spend money on new developments that will provide a new identity, just as Barney urgently wanted. They build new roads, buildings, water features, parks and technology; the town's heart remains the same but cosmetically it is a different place. The visitor is lost, and it becomes unrecognisable.

When a child leaves their home town where they were born and reared, and moves to pastures green, on their return years later they may find that the roads and fields they scurried around as a child no longer exist; only the memories.

Gone is the house where Mother Brown lived, gone is the barber shop, gone is Ken Burton's paper shop, and the roads have changed so much the person who was once a child here does not know how to exit the ring road.

Where are the people who once lived here? Old Mr Hasler who chased you down the road, and promised you a new football if you did not steal the fruit from his trees, and honoured that promise eight months later.

Where have they all gone?!

Our story is a true tale that occurred many years ago. Most of the characters are also gone; some have passed on whilst others have moved on.

African towns, unlike those described above, have changed little – perhaps a new shopping mall; maybe a new church, but those dirty whitewashed walls of the small houses remain the same.

And what about the people in this story – what happened to them?

Charles, alias Barney, alias Edward, is still ducking and diving and avoiding the security forces. He probably always will.

The last that was heard of him he was running a business in County Laois in Ireland, but that was before the 1999 Good Friday Agreement!

Brendan, that wonderful leprechaun, is probably retired from the foundry and living in some sun-drenched land, sipping wine dreaming of his time in Zambia.

Martin finished his contract, and retired from promoting boxing.

Wolfgang continued to live in Kitwe and retained an interest in boxing for a short while, but gave it up after a year to concentrate on his business. He sold up shortly after the millennium, retired, and died two years later.

Musankabala maintained his African title for two years, and during this time he fought and lost in a world title eliminating contest. He died of AIDS shortly after retiring.

Sarah Siddons, the lady let down by Barney, remained single thereafter. Her experience with him taught her never to trust another man, though she still meets with her lady friends just off the Marylebone Road on a weekly basis.

Declan was released after the Good Friday Agreement and immediately started a family with his girlfriend Bridget and now have a family of four.

And Naomi, well, her children are now middle-aged. The oldest boy became a priest, whilst her daughter was educated at

Cambridge and now travels the world representing a well-known charity. Her youngest son became well known in journalism in Southern Africa; his speciality is sport.

George Webster became a director of the Special Operations Executive.

George Mwanza – now, there is a man. I wouldn't say he is a hero or a villain, but without doubt he is an enigma!

And the lovely Naomi? Her whereabouts is unknown but I hope that she is still dancing the night away!

ACKNOWLEDGEMENTS

I would like to pay homage to all those wonderful and not so fortunate people in the pages of my book; they are not cartoon characters, nor an imagination of the mind; but real people.

And to my dear friends Linda and Mike who have given me utmost support, and last but not least to my wonderful wife Pat to whom I extend the deepest love and appreciation.